PEARSON

COMMON CORE

Literature

Close Reading Notebook

THE BRITISH TRADITION

PEARSON

UPPER SADDLE RIVER, NEW JERSEY • BOSTON, MASSACHUSETTS
CHANDLER, ARIZONA • GLENVIEW, ILLINOIS

Acknowledgments appear on page 181, which constitutes an extension of this copyright page.

ISBN-13: 978-0-13-327571-1
ISBN-10:   0-13-327571-X
2 3 4 5 6 7 8 9 10 V039 17 16 15 14 13

CONTENTS

UNIT 1
The Seafarer, translated by Burton Raffel 1
from **Beowulf,** translated by Burton Raffel 5
The Wife of Bath's Tale by Geoffery Chaucer, translated by Nevill Coghill 29
from **Morte d'Arthur** by Sir Thomas Malory 40

UNIT 2
Sonnet 1 by Edmund Spenser 49
Sonnet 35 by Edmund Spenser 50
Sonnet 75 by Edmund Spenser 51
Speech Before Her Troops by Queen Elizabeth I 52
The Tragedy of Macbeth, Act I, by William Shakespeare 54

UNIT 3
Song by John Donne 74
A Valediction: Forbidding Mourning by John Donne 76
Holy Sonnet 10 by John Donne 78
Meditation 17 by John Donne 79
from the **Divine Comedy: Inferno** by Dante Alighieri 81
from **Gulliver's Travels** by Jonathan Swift 87
The Aims of *The Spectator* by Joseph Addison 98

UNIT 4
Introduction to Frankenstein by Mary Wollstonecraft Shelley 101
She Walks in Beauty by George Gordon, Lord Byron 106
from **Childe Harold's Pilgrimage (Apostrophe to the Ocean)** by George
   Gordon, Lord Byron 107
from **Don Juan** by George Gordon, Lord Byron 110
On Making an Agreeable Marriage by Jane Austen 114
from **A Vindication of the Rights of Woman** by Mary Wollstonecraft 118

UNIT 5
My Last Duchess by Robert Browning 121
Life in a Love by Robert Browning 123
Porphyria's Lover by Robert Browning 124
Sonnet 43 by Elizabeth Barrett Browning 126
from **Jane Eyre** by Charlotte Brontë 127
Dover Beach by Matthew Arnold 135
Recessional by Rudyard Kipling 137
The Widow at Windsor by Rudyard Kipling 139
God's Grandeur by Gerard Manley Hopkins 141
Spring and Fall: to a Young Child by Gerard Manley Hopkins 142
To an Athlete Dying Young by A. E. Housman 143
When I Was One-and-Twenty by A. E. Housman 144

CONTENTS

UNIT 6

Sailing to Byzantium by William Butler Yeats 145
The Rocking-Horse Winner by D. H. Lawrence. 147
The Train from Rhodesia by Nadine Gordimer. 163
A Devoted Son by Anita Desai. 167

The Seafarer

Translated by Burton Raffel

TAKE NOTES

BACKGROUND *To the Anglo-Saxon people of Britain, home meant something different from what it means for people today. An Anglo-Saxon warrior viewed himself as the follower of a particular lord or king, not as a citizen of a nation. Gathering in the mead-hall, a building dedicated to their feasts, a lord and his warriors would share food, drink, entertainment, and fellowship. Smoky, noisy, smelly, and crowded, the mead-hall was home.*

This tale is true, and mine. It tells
How the sea took me, swept me back
And forth in sorrow and fear and pain,
Showed me suffering in a hundred ships,
5 In a thousand ports, and in me. It tells
Of smashing surf when I sweated in the cold
Of an anxious watch, perched in the bow
As it dashed under cliffs. My feet were cast
In icy bands, bound with frost,
10 With frozen chains, and hardship groaned
Around my heart. Hunger tore
At my sea-weary soul. No man sheltered
On the quiet fairness of earth can feel
How wretched I was, drifting through winter
15 On an ice-cold sea, whirled in sorrow,
Alone in a world blown clear of love,
Hung with icicles. The hailstorms flew.
The only sound was the roaring sea,
The freezing waves. The song of the swan
20 Might serve for pleasure, the cry of the sea-fowl,
The death-noise of birds instead of laughter,
The mewing of gulls instead of mead.[1]
Storms beat on the rocky cliffs and were echoed
By icy-feathered terns and the eagle's screams;

---

1. mead liquor made from fermented honey and water.

TAKE NOTES

25 No kinsman could offer comfort there,
To a soul left drowning in desolation.
    And who could believe, knowing but
The passion of cities, swelled proud with wine
And no taste of misfortune, how often, how wearily,
30 I put myself back on the paths of the sea.
Night would blacken; it would snow from the north;
Frost bound the earth and hail would fall,
The coldest seeds. And how my heart
Would begin to beat, knowing once more
35 The salt waves tossing and the towering sea!
The time for journeys would come and my soul
Called me eagerly out, sent me over
The horizon, seeking foreigners' homes.
    But there isn't a man on earth so proud,
40 So born to greatness, so bold with his youth,
Grown so brave, or so graced by God,
That he feels no fear as the sails unfurl,
Wondering what Fate has willed and will do.
No harps ring in his heart, no rewards,
45 No passion for women, no worldly pleasures,
Nothing, only the ocean's heave;
But longing wraps itself around him.
Orchards blossom, the towns bloom,
Fields grow lovely as the world springs fresh,
50 And all these admonish that willing mind
Leaping to journeys, always set
In thoughts traveling on a quickening tide.
So summer's sentinel, the cuckoo, sings
In his murmuring voice, and our hearts mourn
55 As he urges. Who could understand,
In ignorant ease, what we others suffer
As the paths of exile stretch endlessly on?
    And yet my heart wanders away,
My soul roams with the sea, the whales'
60 Home, wandering to the widest corners
Of the world, returning ravenous with desire,
Flying solitary, screaming, exciting me
To the open ocean, breaking oaths
On the curve of a wave.
            Thus the joys of God
65 Are fervent with life, where life itself
Fades quickly into the earth. The wealth
Of the world neither reaches to Heaven nor remains.

No man has ever faced the dawn
Certain which of Fate's three threats
70 Would fall: illness, or age, or an enemy's
Sword, snatching the life from his soul.
The praise the living pour on the dead
Flowers from reputation: plant
An earthly life of profit reaped
75 Even from hatred and rancor, of bravery
Flung in the devil's face, and death
Can only bring you earthly praise
And a song to celebrate a place
With the angels, life eternally blessed
80 In the hosts of Heaven.
                    The days are gone
When the kingdoms of earth flourished in glory;
Now there are no rulers, no emperors,
No givers of gold, as once there were,
When wonderful things were worked among them
85 And they lived in lordly magnificence.
Those powers have vanished, those pleasures are
    dead.
The weakest survives and the world continues,
Kept spinning by toil. All glory is tarnished.
The world's honor ages and shrinks,
90 Bent like the men who mold it. Their faces
Blanch as time advances, their beards
Wither and they mourn the memory of friends.
The sons of princes, sown in the dust.
The soul stripped of its flesh knows nothing
95 Of sweetness or sour, feels no pain,
Bends neither its hand nor its brain. A brother
Opens his palms and pours down gold
On his kinsman's grave, strewing his coffin
With treasures intended for Heaven, but nothing
100 Golden shakes the wrath of God
For a soul overflowing with sin, and nothing
Hidden on earth rises to Heaven.
       We all fear God. He turns the earth,
He set it swinging firmly in space,
105 Gave life to the world and light to the sky.
Death leaps at the fools who forget their God.
He who lives humbly has angels from Heaven
To carry him courage and strength and belief.
A man must conquer pride, not kill it,

TAKE NOTES

110 Be firm with his fellows, chaste for himself,
Treat all the world as the world deserves,
With love or with hate but never with harm,
Though an enemy seek to scorch him in hell,
Or set the flames of a funeral pyre
115 Under his lord. Fate is stronger
And God mightier than any man's mind.
Our thoughts should turn to where our home is,
Consider the ways of coming there,
Then strive for sure permission for us
120 To rise to that eternal joy,
That life born in the love of God
And the hope of Heaven. Praise the Holy
Grace of Him who honored us,
Eternal, unchanging creator of earth. Amen.

from **Beowulf**

Translated by Burton Raffel

BACKGROUND *When Beowulf was composed, England was changing from a pagan to a Christian culture. Pagan Anglo-Saxons told grim tales of life ruled by fate, tales in which people struggled against monsters for their place in the world. The missionaries who converted them to Christianity taught them that human beings and their choices of good or evil were at the center of creation. Beowulf reflects both pagan and Christian traditions. The selection opens during an evening of celebration at Herot, the banquet hall of the Danish king Hrothgar (hroth´gär). Outside in the darkness, however, lurks the murderous monster Grendel.*

The Wrath of Grendel

     A powerful monster, living down
In the darkness, growled in pain, impatient
As day after day the music rang
Loud in that hall,[1] the harp's rejoicing
5   Call and the poet's clear songs, sung
Of the ancient beginnings of us all, recalling
The Almighty making the earth, shaping
These beautiful plains marked off by oceans,
Then proudly setting the sun and moon
10 To glow across the land and light it;
The corners of the earth were made lovely with trees
And leaves, made quick with life, with each
Of the nations who now move on its face. And then
As now warriors sang of their pleasure:
15 So Hrothgar's men lived happy in his hall
Till the monster stirred, that demon, that fiend,
Grendel, who haunted the moors, the wild
Marshes, and made his home in a hell
Not hell but earth. He was spawned in that slime,

---

1. hall Herot.

TAKE NOTES

20 Conceived by a pair of those monsters born
Of Cain,[2] murderous creatures banished
By God, punished forever for the crime
Of Abel's death. The Almighty drove
Those demons out, and their exile was bitter,
25 Shut away from men; they split
Into a thousand forms of evil—spirits
And fiends, goblins, monsters, giants,
A brood forever opposing the Lord's
Will, and again and again defeated.
30   Then, when darkness had dropped, Grendel
Went up to Herot, wondering what the warriors
Would do in that hall when their drinking was done.
He found them sprawled in sleep, suspecting
Nothing, their dreams undisturbed. The monster's
35 Thoughts were as quick as his greed or his claws:
He slipped through the door and there in the silence
Snatched up thirty men, smashed them
Unknowing in their beds and ran out with their
    bodies,
The blood dripping behind him, back
40 To his lair, delighted with his night's slaughter.
    At daybreak, with the sun's first light, they saw
How well he had worked, and in that gray morning
Broke their long feast with tears and laments
For the dead. Hrothgar, their lord, sat joyless
45 In Herot, a mighty prince mourning
The fate of his lost friends and companions,
Knowing by its tracks that some demon had torn
His followers apart. He wept, fearing
The beginning might not be the end. And that night
50 Grendel came again, so set
On murder that no crime could ever be enough,
No savage assault quench his lust
For evil. Then each warrior tried
To escape him, searched for rest in different
55 Beds, as far from Herot as they could find,
Seeing how Grendel hunted when they slept.
Distance was safety; the only survivors
Were those who fled him. Hate had triumphed.
    So Grendel ruled, fought with the righteous,

---

2. Cain oldest son of Adam and Eve, who murdered his brother, Abel.

60 One against many, and won; so Herot
Stood empty, and stayed deserted for years,
Twelve winters of grief for Hrothgar, king
Of the Danes, sorrow heaped at his door
By hell-forged hands. His misery leaped
65 The seas, was told and sung in all
Men's ears: how Grendel's hatred began,
How the monster relished his savage war
On the Danes, keeping the bloody feud
Alive, seeking no peace, offering
70 No truce, accepting no settlement, no price
In gold or land, and paying the living
For one crime only with another. No one
Waited for reparation from his plundering claws:
That shadow of death hunted in the darkness,
75 Stalked Hrothgar's warriors, old
And young, lying in waiting, hidden
In mist, invisibly following them from the edge
Of the marsh, always there, unseen.
        So mankind's enemy continued his crimes,
80 Killing as often as he could, coming
Alone, bloodthirsty and horrible. Though he lived
In Herot, when the night hid him, he never
Dared to touch King Hrothgar's glorious
Throne, protected by God—God,
85 Whose love Grendel could not know. But Hrothgar's
Heart was bent. The best and most noble
Of his council debated remedies, sat
In secret sessions, talking of terror
And wondering what the bravest of warriors
        could do.
90 And sometimes they sacrificed to the old stone gods,
Made heathen vows, hoping for Hell's
Support, the Devil's guidance in driving
Their affliction off. That was their way,
And the heathen's only hope, Hell
95 Always in their hearts, knowing neither God
Nor His passing as He walks through our world,
        the Lord
Of Heaven and earth; their ears could not hear
His praise nor know His glory. Let them
Beware, those who are thrust into danger,

TAKE NOTES

100 Clutched at by trouble, yet can carry no solace
In their hearts, cannot hope to be better! Hail
To those who will rise to God, drop off
Their dead bodies and seek our Father's peace!

The Coming of Beowulf

So the living sorrow of Healfdane's son[3]
105 Simmered, bitter and fresh, and no wisdom
Or strength could break it: that agony hung
On king and people alike, harsh
And unending, violent and cruel, and evil.
In his far-off home Beowulf, Higlac's[4]
110 Follower and the strongest of the Geats—greater
And stronger than anyone anywhere in this world—
Heard how Grendel filled nights with horror
And quickly commanded a boat fitted out,
Proclaiming that he'd go to that famous king,
115 Would sail across the sea to Hrothgar,
Now when help was needed. None
Of the wise ones regretted his going, much
As he was loved by the Geats: the omens were
    good,
And they urged the adventure on. So Beowulf
120 Chose the mightiest men he could find,
The bravest and best of the Geats, fourteen
In all, and led them down to their boat;
He knew the sea, would point the prow
Straight to that distant Danish shore.
125   Then they sailed, set their ship
Out on the waves, under the cliffs.
Ready for what came they wound through the
    currents,
The seas beating at the sand, and were borne
In the lap of their shining ship, lined
130 With gleaming armor, going safely
In that oak-hard boat to where their hearts took
    them.
The wind hurried them over the waves,
The ship foamed through the sea like a bird
Until, in the time they had known it would take,

---

3. **Healfdane's** (hä′ alf den′ nez) **son** Hrothgar.
4. **Higlac's** (hig′ laks) Higlac was the king of the Geats (gā′ ats) and Beowulf's feudal lord and uncle.

135 Standing in the round-curled prow they could see
Sparkling hills, high and green
Jutting up over the shore, and rejoicing
In those rock-steep cliffs they quietly ended
Their voyage. Jumping to the ground, the Geats
140 Pushed their boat to the sand and tied it
In place, mail[5] shirts and armor rattling
As they swiftly moored their ship. And then
They gave thanks to God for their easy crossing.
     High on a wall a Danish watcher
145 Patrolling along the cliffs saw
The travelers crossing to the shore, their shields
Raised and shining; he came riding down,
Hrothgar's lieutenant, spurring his horse,
Needing to know why they'd landed, these men
150 In armor. Shaking his heavy spear
In their faces he spoke:
              "Whose soldiers are you,
You who've been carried in your deep-keeled ship
Across the sea-road to this country of mine?
Listen! I've stood on these cliffs longer
155 Than you know, keeping our coast free
Of pirates, raiders sneaking ashore
From their ships, seeking our lives and our gold.
None have ever come more openly—
And yet you've offered no password, no sign
160 From my prince, no permission from my people
   for your landing
Here. Nor have I ever seen,
Out of all the men on earth, one greater
Than has come with you; no commoner carries
Such weapons, unless his appearance, and his
   beauty,
165 Are both lies. You! Tell me your name,
And your father's; no spies go further onto Danish
Soil than you've come already. Strangers,
From wherever it was you sailed, tell it,
And tell it quickly, the quicker the better,
170 I say, for us all. Speak, say
Exactly who you are, and from where, and why."
     Their leader answered him, Beowulf unlocking
Words from deep in his breast:

---

5. **mail** flexible body armor made of metal.

TAKE NOTES

                         "We are Geats,
Men who follow Higlac. My father

175 Was a famous soldier, known far and wide
As a leader of men. His name was Edgetho.
His life lasted many winters;
Wise men all over the earth surely
Remember him still. And we have come seeking

180 Your prince, Healfdane's son, protector
Of this people, only in friendship: instruct us,
Watchman, help us with your words! Our errand
Is a great one, our business with the glorious king
Of the Danes no secret; there's nothing dark

185 Or hidden in our coming. You know (if we've heard
The truth, and been told honestly) that your
    country
Is cursed with some strange, vicious creature
That hunts only at night and that no one
Has seen. It's said, watchman, that he has
    slaughtered

190 Your people, brought terror to the darkness. Perhaps
Hrothgar can hunt, here in my heart,
For some way to drive this devil out—
If anything will ever end the evils
Afflicting your wise and famous lord.

195 Here he can cool his burning sorrow.
Or else he may see his suffering go on
Forever, for as long as Herot towers
High on your hills."

                    The mounted officer
Answered him bluntly, the brave watchman:

200   "A soldier should know the difference between
    words
And deeds, and keep that knowledge clear
In his brain. I believe your words, I trust in
Your friendship. Go forward, weapons and armor
And all, on into Denmark. I'll guide you

205 Myself—and my men will guard your ship,
Keep it safe here on our shores,
Your fresh-tarred boat, watch it well,
Until that curving prow carries
Across the sea to Geatland a chosen

210 Warrior who bravely does battle with the creature
Haunting our people, who survives that horror
Unhurt, and goes home bearing our love."

Then they moved on. Their boat lay moored,
Tied tight to its anchor. Glittering at the top
215 Of their golden helmets wild boar heads gleamed,
Shining decorations, swinging as they marched,
Erect like guards, like sentinels, as though ready
To fight. They marched, Beowulf and his men
And their guide, until they could see the gables
220 Of Herot, covered with hammered gold
And glowing in the sun—that most famous of
   all dwellings,
Towering majestic, its glittering roofs
Visible far across the land.
Their guide reined in his horse, pointing
225 To that hall, built by Hrothgar for the best
And bravest of his men; the path was plain,
They could see their way. . . .

*Beowulf and his men arrive at Herot and are called
to see the King.*

              Beowulf arose, with his men
230 Around him, ordering a few to remain
With their weapons, leading the others quickly
Along under Herot's steep roof into Hrothgar's
Presence. Standing on that prince's own hearth,
Helmeted, the silvery metal of his mail shirt
235 Gleaming with a smith's high art, he greeted
The Danes' great lord:
              "Hail, Hrothgar!
Higlac is my cousin[6] and my king; the days
Of my youth have been filled with glory. Now
   Grendel's
Name has echoed in our land: sailors
240 Have brought us stories of Herot, the best
Of all mead-halls,[7] deserted and useless when the
   moon
Hangs in skies the sun had lit,
Light and life fleeing together.
My people have said, the wisest, most knowing
245 And best of them, that my duty was to go to the
   Danes'

---

6. **cousin** here, used as a general term for relative.
7. **mead-halls** To reward his thanes, the king in heroic literature would build a hall
   where mead (a drink made from fermented honey) was served.

TAKE NOTES

Great king. They have seen my strength for
   themselves,
Have watched me rise from the darkness of war,
Dripping with my enemies' blood. I drove
Five great giants into chains, chased
250 All of that race from the earth. I swam
In the blackness of night, hunting monsters
Out of the ocean, and killing them one
By one; death was my errand and the fate
They had earned. Now Grendel and I are called
255 Together, and I've come. Grant me, then,
Lord and protector of this noble place,
A single request! I have come so far,
O shelterer of warriors and your people's loved
   friend,
That this one favor you should not refuse me—
260 That I, alone and with the help of my men,
May purge all evil from this hall. I have heard,
Too, that the monster's scorn of men
Is so great that he needs no weapons and fears
   none.
Nor will I. My lord Higlac
265 Might think less of me if I let my sword
Go where my feet were afraid to, if I hid
Behind some broad linden[8] shield: my hands
Alone shall fight for me, struggle for life
Against the monster. God must decide
270 Who will be given to death's cold grip.
Grendel's plan, I think, will be
What it has been before, to invade this hall
And gorge his belly with our bodies. If he can,
If he can. And I think, if my time will have come,
275 There'll be nothing to mourn over, no corpse to
   prepare
For its grave: Grendel will carry our bloody
Flesh to the moors, crunch on our bones
And smear torn scraps of our skin on the walls
Of his den. No, I expect no Danes
280 Will fret about sewing our shrouds, if he wins.
And if death does take me, send the hammered
Mail of my armor to Higlac, return

---

8. **linden** very sturdy type of wood.

The inheritance I had from Hrethel, and he
From Wayland.[9] Fate will unwind as it must!"

That night Beowulf and his men stay inside Herot.
While his men sleep, Beowulf lies awake, eager to
meet with Grendel.

The Battle with Grendel

285   Out from the marsh, from the foot of misty
Hills and bogs, bearing God's hatred,
Grendel came, hoping to kill
Anyone he could trap on this trip to high Herot.
He moved quickly through the cloudy night,
290 Up from his swampland, sliding silently
Toward that gold-shining hall. He had visited
   Hrothgar's
Home before, knew the way—
But never, before nor after that night,
Found Herot defended so firmly, his reception
295 So harsh. He journeyed, forever joyless,
Straight to the door, then snapped it open,
Tore its iron fasteners with a touch
And rushed angrily over the threshold.
He strode quickly across the inlaid
300 Floor, snarling and fierce: his eyes
Gleamed in the darkness, burned with a gruesome
Light. Then he stopped, seeing the hall
Crowded with sleeping warriors, stuffed
With rows of young soldiers resting together.
305 And his heart laughed, he relished the sight,
Intended to tear the life from those bodies
By morning; the monster's mind was hot
With the thought of food and the feasting his belly
Would soon know. But fate, that night, intended
310 Grendel to gnaw the broken bones
Of his last human supper. Human
Eyes were watching his evil steps,
Waiting to see his swift hard claws.
Grendel snatched at the first Geat
315 He came to, ripped him apart, cut
His body to bits with powerful jaws,
Drank the blood from his veins and bolted

---

9. **Wayland** from Germanic folklore, an invisible blacksmith.

TAKE NOTES

____

____

____

____

____

____

____

____

____

____

____

____

____

____

____

____

____

____

____

____

Him down, hands and feet; death
And Grendel's great teeth came together,
320 Snapping life shut. Then he stepped to another
Still body, clutched at Beowulf with his claws,
Grasped at a strong-hearted wakeful sleeper
—And was instantly seized himself, claws
Bent back as Beowulf leaned up on one arm.
325   That shepherd of evil, guardian of crime,
Knew at once that nowhere on earth
Had he met a man whose hands were harder;
His mind was flooded with fear—but nothing
Could take his talons and himself from that tight
330 Hard grip. Grendel's one thought was to run
From Beowulf, flee back to his marsh and hide
    there:
This was a different Herot than the hall he had
    emptied.
But Higlac's follower remembered his final
Boast and, standing erect, stopped
335 The monster's flight, fastened those claws
In his fists till they cracked, clutched Grendel
Closer. The infamous killer fought
For his freedom, wanting no flesh but retreat,
Desiring nothing but escape; his claws
340 Had been caught, he was trapped. That trip to
    Herot
Was a miserable journey for the writhing monster!
    The high hall rang, its roof boards swayed,
And Danes shook with terror. Down
The aisles the battle swept, angry
345 And wild. Herot trembled, wonderfully
Built to withstand the blows, the struggling
Great bodies beating at its beautiful walls;
Shaped and fastened with iron, inside
And out, artfully worked, the building
350 Stood firm. Its benches rattled, fell
To the floor, gold-covered boards grating
As Grendel and Beowulf battled across them.
Hrothgar's wise men had fashioned Herot
To stand forever; only fire,
355 They had planned, could shatter what such skill
    had put
Together, swallow in hot flames such splendor
Of ivory and iron and wood. Suddenly

The sounds changed, the Danes started
In new terror, cowering in their beds as the terrible
360 Screams of the Almighty's enemy sang
In the darkness, the horrible shrieks of pain
And defeat, the tears torn out of Grendel's
Taut throat, hell's captive caught in the arms
Of him who of all the men on earth
365 Was the strongest.

                   That mighty protector of men
Meant to hold the monster till its life
Leaped out, knowing the fiend was no use
To anyone in Denmark. All of Beowulf's
Band had jumped from their beds, ancestral
370 Swords raised and ready, determined
To protect their prince if they could. Their courage
Was great but all wasted: they could hack at
    Grendel
From every side, trying to open
A path for his evil soul, but their points
375 Could not hurt him, the sharpest and hardest iron
Could not scratch at his skin, for that sin-stained
    demon
Had bewitched all men's weapons, laid spells
That blunted every mortal man's blade.
And yet his time had come, his days
380 Were over, his death near; down
To hell he would go, swept groaning and helpless
To the waiting hands of still worse fiends.
Now he discovered—once the afflictor
Of men, tormentor of their days—what it meant
385 To feud with Almighty God: Grendel
Saw that his strength was deserting him, his claws
Bound fast, Higlac's brave follower tearing at
His hands. The monster's hatred rose higher,
But his power had gone. He twisted in pain,
390 And the bleeding sinews deep in his shoulder
Snapped, muscle and bone split
And broke. The battle was over, Beowulf
Had been granted new glory: Grendel escaped,
But wounded as he was could flee to his den,
395 His miserable hole at the bottom of the marsh,
Only to die, to wait for the end
Of all his days. And after that bloody
Combat the Danes laughed with delight.
He who had come to them from across the sea,

TAKE NOTES

400 Bold and strong-minded, had driven affliction
Off, purged Herot clean. He was happy,
Now, with that night's fierce work; the Danes
Had been served as he'd boasted he'd serve them;
  Beowulf,
A prince of the Geats, had killed Grendel,
405 Ended the grief, the sorrow, the suffering
Forced on Hrothgar's helpless people
By a bloodthirsty fiend. No Dane doubted
The victory, for the proof, hanging high
From the rafters where Beowulf had hung it, was
  the monster's
410 Arm, claw and shoulder and all.

The Danes celebrate Beowulf's victory. That night,
though, Grendel's mother kills Hrothgar's closest
friend and carries off her child's claw. The next
day the horrified king tells Beowulf about the two
monsters and their underwater lair.

The Monsters' Lair

  "I've heard that my people, peasants working
In the fields, have seen a pair of such fiends
Wandering in the moors and marshes, giant
Monsters living in those desert lands.
415 And they've said to my wise men that, as well as
  they could see,
One of the devils was a female creature.
The other, they say, walked through the wilderness
Like a man—but mightier than any man.
They were frightened, and they fled, hoping to
  find help
420 In Herot. They named the huge one Grendel:
If he had a father no one knew him,
Or whether there'd been others before these two,
Hidden evil before hidden evil.
They live in secret places, windy
425 Cliffs, wolf-dens where water pours
From the rocks, then runs underground, where
  mist
Steams like black clouds, and the groves of trees
Growing out over their lake are all covered
With frozen spray, and wind down snakelike

430 Roots that reach as far as the water
    And help keep it dark. At night that lake
    Burns like a torch. No one knows its bottom,
    No wisdom reaches such depths. A deer,
    Hunted through the woods by packs of hounds,
435 A stag with great horns, though driven through
        the forest
    From faraway places, prefers to die
    On those shores, refuses to save its life
    In that water. It isn't far, nor is it
    A pleasant spot! When the wind stirs
440 And storms, waves splash toward the sky,
    As dark as the air, as black as the rain
    That the heavens weep. Our only help,
    Again, lies with you. Grendel's mother
    Is hidden in her terrible home, in a place
445 You've not seen. Seek it, if you dare! Save us,
    Once more, and again twisted gold,
    Heaped-up ancient treasure, will reward you
    For the battle you win!"

Beowulf resolves to kill Grendel's monstrous mother.
He travels to the lake in which she lives.

The Battle with Grendel's Mother

    Then Edgetho's brave son[10] spoke:
                                "Remember,
450 Hrothgar, O knowing king, now
    When my danger is near, the warm words we
        uttered,
    And if your enemy should end my life
    Then be, O generous prince, forever
    The father and protector of all whom I leave
455 Behind me, here in your hands, my beloved
    Comrades left with no leader, their leader
    Dead. And the precious gifts you gave me,
    My friend, send them to Higlac. May he see
    In their golden brightness, the Geats' great lord
460 Gazing at your treasure, that here in Denmark
    I found a noble protector, a giver
    Of rings whose rewards I won and briefly

---

10. Edgetho's brave son Beowulf. Elsewhere he is identified by such phrases as "the Geats' proud prince" and "the Geats' brave prince."

TAKE NOTES

Relished. And you, Unferth,[11] let
My famous old sword stay in your hands:
465 I shall shape glory with Hrunting, or death
Will hurry me from this earth!"

As his words ended
He leaped into the lake, would not wait for anyone's
Answer; the heaving water covered him
Over. For hours he sank through the waves;
470 At last he saw the mud of the bottom.
And all at once the greedy she-wolf
Who'd ruled those waters for half a hundred
Years discovered him, saw that a creature
From above had come to explore the bottom
475 Of her wet world. She welcomed him in her claws,
Clutched at him savagely but could not harm him,
Tried to work her fingers through the tight
Ring-woven mail on his breast, but tore
And scratched in vain. Then she carried him, armor
480 And sword and all, to her home; he struggled
To free his weapon, and failed. The fight
Brought other monsters swimming to see
Her catch, a host of sea beasts who beat at
His mail shirt, stabbing with tusks and teeth
485 As they followed along. Then he realized, suddenly,
That she'd brought him into someone's battle-hall,
And there the water's heat could not hurt him.
Nor anything in the lake attack him through
The building's high-arching roof. A brilliant
490 Light burned all around him, the lake
Itself like a fiery flame.

Then he saw
The mighty water witch and swung his sword,
His ring-marked blade, straight at her head;
The iron sang its fierce song,
495 Sang Beowulf's strength. But her guest
Discovered that no sword could slice her evil
Skin, that Hrunting could not hurt her, was
 useless
Now when he needed it. They wrestled, she ripped
And tore and clawed at him, bit holes in his helmet,
500 And that too failed him; for the first time in years
Of being worn to war it would earn no glory;

---

11. **Unferth** Danish warrior who had questioned Beowulf's bravery before the
battle with Grendel.

It was the last time anyone would wear it. But
        Beowulf
Longed only for fame, leaped back
Into battle. He tossed his sword aside,
505 Angry; the steel-edged blade lay where
He'd dropped it. If weapons were useless he'd use
His hands, the strength in his fingers. So fame
Comes to the men who mean to win it
And care about nothing else! He raised
510 His arms and seized her by the shoulder; anger
Doubled his strength, he threw her to the floor.
She fell, Grendel's fierce mother, and the Geats'
Proud prince was ready to leap on her. But she
        rose
At once and repaid him with her clutching claws,
515 Wildly tearing at him. He was weary, that best
And strongest of soldiers; his feet stumbled
And in an instant she had him down, held helpless.
Squatting with her weight on his stomach, she
        drew
A dagger, brown with dried blood, and prepared
520 To avenge her only son. But he was stretched
On his back, and her stabbing blade was blunted
By the woven mail shirt he wore on his chest.
The hammered links held; the point
Could not touch him. He'd have traveled to the
        bottom of the earth,
525 Edgetho's son, and died there, if that shining
Woven metal had not helped—and Holy
God, who sent him victory, gave judgment
For truth and right, Ruler of the Heavens,
Once Beowulf was back on his feet and fighting.
530   Then he saw, hanging on the wall, a heavy
Sword, hammered by giants, strong
And blessed with their magic, the best of all
        weapons
But so massive that no ordinary man could lift
Its carved and decorated length. He drew it
535 From its scabbard, broke the chain on its hilt,
And then, savage, now, angry
And desperate, lifted it high over his head
And struck with all the strength he had left,
Caught her in the neck and cut it through,

TAKE NOTES

540 Broke bones and all. Her body fell
To the floor, lifeless, the sword was wet
With her blood, and Beowulf rejoiced at the sight.
    The brilliant light shone, suddenly,
As though burning in that hall, and as bright as
    Heaven's
545 Own candle, lit in the sky. He looked
At her home, then following along the wall
Went walking, his hands tight on the sword,
His heart still angry. He was hunting another
Dead monster, and took his weapon with him
550 For final revenge against Grendel's vicious
Attacks, his nighttime raids, over
And over, coming to Herot when Hrothgar's
Men slept, killing them in their beds,
Eating some on the spot, fifteen
555 Or more, and running to his loathsome moor
With another such sickening meal waiting
In his pouch. But Beowulf repaid him for those
    visits,
Found him lying dead in his corner,
Armless, exactly as that fierce fighter
560 Had sent him out from Herot, then struck off
His head with a single swift blow. The body
jerked for the last time, then lay still.
    The wise old warriors who surrounded
        Hrothgar,
Like him staring into the monsters' lake,
565 Saw the waves surging and blood
Spurting through. They spoke about Beowulf,
All the graybeards, whispered together
And said that hope was gone, that the hero
Had lost fame and his life at once, and would never
570 Return to the living, come back as triumphant
As he had left; almost all agreed that Grendel's
Mighty mother, the she-wolf, had killed him.
The sun slid over past noon, went further
Down. The Danes gave up, left
575 The lake and went home, Hrothgar with them.
The Geats stayed, sat sadly, watching,
Imagining they saw their lord but not believing
They would ever see him again.
                    —Then the sword
Melted, blood-soaked, dripping down

580 Like water, disappearing like ice when the world's
Eternal Lord loosens invisible
Fetters and unwinds icicles and frost
As only He can, He who rules
Time and seasons, He who is truly
585 God. The monsters' hall was full of
Rich treasures, but all that Beowulf took
Was Grendel's head and the hilt of the giants'
Jeweled sword; the rest of that ring-marked
Blade had dissolved in Grendel's steaming
590 Blood, boiling even after his death.
And then the battle's only survivor
Swam up and away from those silent corpses;
The water was calm and clean, the whole
Huge lake peaceful once the demons who'd lived
    in it
595 Were dead.
        Then that noble protector of all seamen
Swam to land, rejoicing in the heavy
Burdens he was bringing with him. He
And all his glorious band of Geats
Thanked God that their leader had come back
    unharmed;
600 They left the lake together. The Geats
Carried Beowulf's helmet, and his mail shirt.
Behind them the water slowly thickened
As the monsters' blood came seeping up.
They walked quickly, happily, across
605 Roads all of them remembered, left
The lake and the cliffs alongside it, brave men
Staggering under the weight of Grendel's skull,
Too heavy for fewer than four of them to handle—
Two on each side of the spear jammed through it—
610 Yet proud of their ugly load and determined
That the Danes, seated in Herot, should see it.
Soon, fourteen Geats arrived
At the hall, bold and warlike, and with Beowulf,
Their lord and leader, they walked on the mead-hall
615 Green. Then the Geats' brave prince entered
Herot, covered with glory for the daring
Battles he had fought; he sought Hrothgar
To salute him and show Grendel's head.
He carried that terrible trophy by the hair,

TAKE NOTES

620 Brought it straight to where the Danes sat,
Drinking, the queen among them. It was a weird
And wonderful sight, and the warriors stared.

*After being honored by Hrothgar, Beowulf and his
fellow Geats return home, where he eventually
becomes King. Beowulf rules Geatland for fifty years.
When a dragon menaces his kingdom, Beowulf, now
an old man, determines to slay the beast. Before
going into battle, he tells his men about the royal
house and his exploits in its service.*

The Last Battle

And Beowulf uttered his final boast:
"I've never known fear, as a youth I fought
625 In endless battles. I am old, now,
But I will fight again, seek fame still,
If the dragon hiding in his tower dares
To face me."
        Then he said farewell to his followers,
Each in his turn, for the last time:
630   "I'd use no sword, no weapon, if this beast
Could be killed without it, crushed to death
Like Grendel, gripped in my hands and torn
Limb from limb. But his breath will be burning
Hot, poison will pour from his tongue.
635 I feel no shame, with shield and sword
And armor, against this monster: when he comes
   to me
I mean to stand, not run from his shooting
Flames, stand till fate decides
Which of us wins. My heart is firm,
640 My hands calm: I need no hot
Words. Wait for me close by, my friends.
We shall see, soon, who will survive
This bloody battle, stand when the fighting
Is done. No one else could do
645 What I mean to, here, no man but me
Could hope to defeat this monster. No one
Could try. And this dragon's treasure, his gold
And everything hidden in that tower, will be mine
Or war will sweep me to a bitter death!"

650   Then Beowulf rose, still brave, still strong,
And with his shield at his side, and a mail shirt on
    his breast,
Strode calmly, confidently, toward the tower, under
The rocky cliffs: no coward could have walked
    there!
And then he who'd endured dozens of desperate
655 Battles, who'd stand boldly while swords and
    shields
Clashed, the best of kings, saw
Huge stone arches and felt the heat
Of the dragon's breath, flooding down
Through the hidden entrance, too hot for anyone
660 To stand, a streaming current of fire
And smoke that blocked all passage. And the Geats'
Lord and leader, angry, lowered
His sword and roared out a battle cry,
A call so loud and clear that it reached through
665 The hoary rock, hung in the dragon's
Ear. The beast rose, angry,
Knowing a man had come—and then nothing
But war could have followed. Its breath came first.
A steaming cloud pouring from the stone,
670 Then the earth itself shook. Beowulf
Swung his shield into place, held it
In front of him, facing the entrance. The dragon
Coiled and uncoiled, its heart urging it
Into battle. Beowulf's ancient sword
675 Was waiting, unsheathed, his sharp and gleaming
Blade. The beast came closer; both of them
Were ready, each set on slaughter. The Geats'
Great prince stood firm, unmoving, prepared
Behind his high shield, waiting in his shining
680 Armor. The monster came quickly toward him,
Pouring out fire and smoke, hurrying
To its fate. Flames beat at the iron
Shield, and for a time it held, protected
Beowulf as he'd planned; then it began to melt,
685 And for the first time in his life that famous prince
Fought with fate against him, with glory
Denied him. He knew it, but he raised his sword
And struck at the dragon's scaly hide.
The ancient blade broke, bit into

TAKE NOTES

TAKE NOTES

690 The monster's skin, drew blood, but cracked
And failed him before it went deep enough, helped
   him
Less than he needed. The dragon leaped
With pain, thrashed and beat at him, spouting
Murderous flames, spreading them everywhere.
695 And the Geats' ring-giver did not boast of glorious
Victories in other wars: his weapon
Had failed him, deserted him, now when he
   needed it
Most, that excellent sword. Edgetho's
Famous son stared at death,
700 Unwilling to leave this world, to exchange it
For a dwelling in some distant place—a journey
Into darkness that all men must make, as death
Ends their few brief hours on earth.
      Quickly, the dragon came at him, encouraged
705 As Beowulf fell back; its breath flared,
And he suffered, wrapped around in swirling
Flames—a king, before, but now
A beaten warrior. None of his comrades
Came to him, helped him, his brave and noble
710 Followers; they ran for their lives, fled
Deep in a wood. And only one of them
Remained, stood there, miserable, remembering,
As a good man must, what kinship should mean.

      His name was Wiglaf, he was Wexstan's son
715 And a good soldier; his family had been Swedish,
Once. Watching Beowulf, he could see
How his king was suffering, burning. Remembering
Everything his lord and cousin had given him,
Armor and gold and the great estates
720 Wexstan's family enjoyed, Wiglaf's
Mind was made up; he raised his yellow
Shield and drew his sword—an ancient
Weapon that had once belonged to Onela's
Nephew, and that Wexstan had won, killing
725 The prince when he fled from Sweden, sought
   safety
With Herdred, and found death.[12] And Wiglaf's
   father

---

12. Onela's / Nephew . . . found death When Onela seized the throne of Sweden, his two nephews sought shelter with the king of Geatland, Herdred. Wiglaf's father, Wexstan, killed the older nephew for Onela.

Had carried the dead man's armor, and his sword,
To Onela, and the king had said nothing, only
Given him armor and sword and all,
730 Everything his rebel nephew had owned
And lost when he left this life. And Wexstan
Had kept those shining gifts, held them
For years, waiting for his son to use them,
Wear them as honorably and well as once
735 His father had done; then Wexstan died
And Wiglaf was his heir, inherited treasures
And weapons and land. He'd never worn
That armor, fought with that sword, until Beowulf
Called him to his side, led him into war.
740 But his soul did not melt, his sword was strong;
The dragon discovered his courage, and his
        weapon,
When the rush of battle brought them together.
    And Wiglaf, his heart heavy, uttered
The kind of words his comrades deserved:
745   "I remember how we sat in the mead-hall,
        drinking
And boasting of how brave we'd be when Beowulf
Needed us, he who gave us these swords
And armor: all of us swore to repay him,
When the time came, kindness for kindness
750 —With our lives, if he needed them. He allowed us
        to join him,
Chose us from all his great army, thinking
Our boasting words had some weight, believing
Our promises, trusting our swords. He took us
For soldiers, for men. He meant to kill
755 This monster himself, our mighty king,
Fight this battle alone and unaided,
As in the days when his strength and daring
        dazzled
Men's eyes. But those days are over and gone
And now our lord must lean on younger
760 Arms. And we must go to him, while angry
Flames burn at his flesh, help
Our glorious king! By almighty God,
I'd rather burn myself than see
Flames swirling around my lord.

TAKE NOTES

765 And who are we to carry home
Our shields before we've slain his enemy
And ours, to run back to our homes with Beowulf
So hard-pressed here? I swear that nothing
He ever did deserved an end
770 Like this, dying miserably and alone,
Butchered by this savage beast: we swore
That these swords and armor were each for us all!"
　　　Then he ran to his king, crying encouragement
As he dove through the dragon's deadly fumes.

Wiglaf and Beowulf kill the dragon, but the old king is mortally wounded. As he dies, Beowulf asks Wiglaf to bring him the treasure that the dragon was guarding.

The Spoils

775　　Then Wexstan's son went in, as quickly
As he could, did as the dying Beowulf
Asked, entered the inner darkness
Of the tower, went with his mail shirt and his
　　sword.
Flushed with victory he groped his way,
780 A brave young warrior, and suddenly saw
Piles of gleaming gold, precious
Gems, scattered on the floor, cups
And bracelets, rusty old helmets, beautifully
Made but rotting with no hands to rub
785 And polish them. They lay where the dragon left
　　them;
It had flown in the darkness, once, before fighting
Its final battle. (So gold can easily
Triumph, defeat the strongest of men,
No matter how deep it is hidden!) And he saw,
790 Hanging high above, a golden
Banner, woven by the best of weavers
And beautiful. And over everything he saw
A strange light, shining everywhere,
On walls and floor and treasure. Nothing
795 Moved, no other monsters appeared;
He took what he wanted, all the treasures
That pleased his eye, heavy plates
And golden cups and the glorious banner,
Loaded his arms with all they could hold.

800 Beowulf's dagger, his iron blade,
Had finished the fire-spitting terror
That once protected tower and treasures
Alike; the gray-bearded lord of the Geats
Had ended those flying, burning raids
805 Forever.
        Then Wiglaf went back, anxious
To return while Beowulf was alive, to bring him
Treasure they'd won together. He ran,
Hoping his wounded king, weak
And dying, had not left the world too soon.
810 Then he brought their treasure to Beowulf, and
    found
His famous king bloody, gasping
For breath. But Wiglaf sprinkled water
Over his lord, until the words
Deep in his breast broke through and were heard.
815 Beholding the treasure he spoke, haltingly:
    "For this, this gold, these jewels, I thank
Our Father in Heaven, Ruler of the Earth—
For all of this, that His grace has given me,
Allowed me to bring to my people while breath
820 Still came to my lips. I sold my life
For this treasure, and I sold it well. Take
What I leave, Wiglaf, lead my people,
Help them; my time is gone. Have
The brave Geats build me a tomb,
825 When the funeral flames have burned me, and
    build it
Here, at the water's edge, high
On this spit of land, so sailors can see
This tower, and remember my name, and call it
Beowulf's tower, and boats in the darkness
830 And mist, crossing the sea, will know it."
    Then that brave king gave the golden
Necklace from around his throat to Wiglaf,
Gave him his gold-covered helmet, and his rings,
And his mail shirt, and ordered him to use them
    well:
835   "You're the last of all our far-flung family.
Fate has swept our race away,
Taken warriors in their strength and led them
To the death that was waiting. And now I follow
    them."
    The old man's mouth was silent, spoke

TAKE NOTES

840 No more, had said as much as it could;
He would sleep in the fire, soon. His soul
Left his flesh, flew to glory.

Wiglaf denounces the warriors who deserted
Beowulf. The Geats burn their king's body on a
funeral pyre and bitterly lament his death.

The Farewell

Then the Geats built the tower, as Beowulf
Had asked, strong and tall, so sailors
845 Could find it from far and wide; working
For ten long days they made his monument,
Sealed his ashes in walls as straight
And high as wise and willing hands
Could raise them. And the riches he and Wiglaf
850 Had won from the dragon, rings, necklaces,
Ancient, hammered armor—all
The treasures they'd taken were left there, too,
Silver and jewels buried in the sandy
Ground, back in the earth, again
855 And forever hidden and useless to men.
And then twelve of the bravest Geats
Rode their horses around the tower,
Telling their sorrow, telling stories
Of their dead king and his greatness, his glory,
860 Praising him for heroic deeds, for a life
As noble as his name. So should all men
Raise up words for their lords, warm
With love, when their shield and protector leaves
His body behind, sends his soul
865 On high. And so Beowulf's followers
Rode, mourning their beloved leader,
Crying that no better king had ever
Lived, no prince so mild, no man
So open to his people, so deserving of praise.

The Wife of Bath's Tale

by Geoffrey Chaucer

translated by Nevill Coghill

When good King Arthur ruled in ancient days,
(A king that every Briton loves to praise.)
This was a land brim-full of fairy folk.
The Elf-Queen and her courtiers joined and broke
5 Their elfin dance on many a green mead,
Or so was the opinion once, I read,
Hundreds of years ago, in days of yore.
But no one now sees fairies any more.
For now the saintly charity and prayer
10 Of holy friars seem to have purged the air;
They search the countryside through field and
   stream
As thick as motes[1] that speckle a sun-beam,
Blessing the halls, the chambers, kitchens, bowers,
Cities and boroughs, castles, courts and towers,
15 Thorpes,[2] barns and stables, outhouses and
   dairies,
And that's the reason why there are no fairies.
Wherever there was wont to walk an elf
To-day there walks the holy friar himself
As evening falls or when the daylight springs,
20 Saying his matins[3] and his holy things,
Walking his limit round from town to town.
Women can now go safely up and down.
By every bush or under every tree;
There is no other incubus but he,
25 So there is really no one else to hurt you
And he will do no more than take your virtue.
      Now it so happened, I began to say,
Long, long ago in good King Arthur's day,
There was a knight who was a lusty liver.
30 One day as he came riding from the river
He saw a maiden walking all forlorn
Ahead of him, alone as she was born.

---

1. **motes** dust particles.
2. **Thorpes** villages.
3. **matins** morning prayers.

TAKE NOTES

And of that maiden, spite of all she said,
By very force he took her maidenhead.
35   This act of violence made such a stir,
So much petitioning of the king for her,
That he condemned the knight to lose his head
By course of law. He was as good as dead
(It seems that then the statutes took that view)
40 But that the queen, and other ladies too,
implored the king to exercise his grace
So ceaselessly, he gave the queen the case
And granted her his life, and she could choose
Whether to show him mercy or refuse.
45   The queen returned him thanks with all her
      might,
And then she sent a summons to the knight
At her convenience, and expressed her will:
"You stand, for such is the position still,
In no way certain of your life," said she,
50 "Yet you shall live if you can answer me:
What is the thing that women most desire?
Beware the axe and say as I require.
    "If you can't answer on the moment, though,
I will concede you this: you are to go
55 A twelvemonth and a day to seek and learn
Sufficient answer, then you shall return.
I shall take gages[4] from you to extort
Surrender of your body to the court."
    Sad was the knight and sorrowfully sighed,
60 But there! All other choices were denied,
And in the end he chose to go away
And to return after a year and day
Armed with such answer as there might be sent
To him by God. He took his leave and went.

65   He knocked at every house, searched every
      place,
Yes, anywhere that offered hope of grace.
What could it be that women wanted most?
But all the same he never touched a coast,
Country or town in which there seemed to be

---

4. **gages** guarantees.

70 Any two people willing to agree.
    Some said that women wanted wealth and
      treasure,
"Honor," said some, some "Jollity and pleasure,"
Some "Gorgeous clothes" and others "Fun in bed,"
" To be oft widowed and remarried," said
75 Others again, and some that what most mattered
Was that we should be cossetted[5] and flattered.
That's very near the truth, it seems to me;
A man can win us best with flattery.
To dance attendance on us, make a fuss,
80 Ensnares us all, the best and worst of us.
    Some say the things we most desire are these:
Freedom to do exactly as we please,
With no one to reprove our faults and lies,
Rather to have one call us good and wise.
85 Truly there's not a woman in ten score
Who has a fault, and someone rubs the sore,
But she will kick if what he says is true;
You try it out and you will find so too.
However vicious we may be within
90 We like to be thought wise and void of sin.
Others assert we women find it sweet
When we are thought dependable, discreet
And secret, firm of purpose and controlled,
Never betraying things that we are told.
95 But that's not worth the handle of a rake;
Women conceal a thing? For Heaven's sake!
Remember Midas?[6] Will you hear the tale?
    Among some other little things, now stale,
Ovid **relates** that under his long hair
100 The unhappy Midas grew a splendid pair
Of ass's ears; as subtly as he might,
He kept his foul deformity from sight;
Save for his wife, there was not one that knew.
He loved her best, and trusted in her too.
105 He begged her not to tell a living creature
That he possessed so horrible a feature.
And she—she swore, were all the world to win,
She would not do such villainy and sin
As saddle her husband with so foul a name;

---

5. **cossetted** pampered.
6. **Midas** In mythology, King Midas had the magic touch that turned everything to
gold. Here, Chaucer makes reference to Ovid's *Metamorphoses*.

TAKE NOTES

110 Besides to speak would be to share the shame.
Nevertheless she thought she would have died
Keeping this secret bottled up inside;
It seemed to swell her heart and she, no doubt,
Thought it was on the point of bursting out.
115　Fearing to speak of it to woman or man,
Down to a reedy marsh she quickly ran
And reached the sedge. Her heart was all on fire
And, as a bittern[7] bumbles in the mire,
She whispered to the water, near the ground,
120 "Betray me not, O water, with thy sound!
To thee alone I tell it: it appears
My husband has a pair of ass's ears!
Ah! My heart's well again, the secret's out!
I could no longer keep it, not a doubt."
125 And so you see, although we may hold fast
A little while, it must come out at last,
We can't keep secrets; as for Midas, well,
Read Ovid for his story; he will tell.
　This knight that I am telling you about
130 Perceived at last he never would find out
What it could be that women loved the best.
Faint was the soul within his sorrowful breast
As home he went, he dared no longer stay;
His year was up and now it was the day.
135　As he rode home in a dejected mood
Suddenly, at the margin of a wood,
He saw a dance upon the leafy floor
Of four and twenty ladies, nay, and more.
Eagerly he approached, in hope to learn
140 Some words of wisdom ere he should return;
But lo! Before he came to where they were,
Dancers and dance all vanished into air!
There wasn't a living creature to be seen
Save one old woman crouched upon the green.
145 A fouler-looking creature I suppose
Could scarcely be imagined. She arose
And said, "Sir knight, there's no way on from here.
Tell me what you are looking for, my dear,
For peradventure that were best for you;
150 We old, old women know a thing or two."
　"Dear Mother," said the knight, "alack the day!

---

7. bittern small wading bird.

I am as good as dead if I can't say
What thing it is that women most desire;
If you could tell me I would pay your hire."
155 "Give me your hand," she said, "and swear to do
Whatever I shall next require of you
—If so to do should lie within your might—
And you shall know the answer before night."
"Upon my honor," he answered, "I agree."
160 "Then," said the crone, "I dare to guarantee
Your life is safe; I shall make good my claim.
Upon my life the queen will say the same.
Show me the very proudest of them all
In costly coverchief or jewelled caul[8]
165 That dare say no to what I have to teach.
Let us go forward without further speech."
And then she crooned her gospel in his ear
And told him to be glad and not to fear.
    They came to court. This knight, in full array,
170 Stood forth and said, "O Queen, I've kept my day
And kept my word and have my answer ready."
    There sat the noble matrons and the heady
Young girls, and widows too, that have the grace
Of wisdom, all assembled in that place,
175 And there the queen herself was throned to hear
And judge his answer. Then the knight drew near
And silence was commanded through the hall.
    The queen then bade the knight to tell them all
What thing it was that women wanted most.
180 He stood not silent like a beast or post,
But gave his answer with the ringing word
Of a man's voice and the assembly heard:
    "My liege and lady, in general," said he,
"A woman wants the self-same sovereignty
185 Over her husband as over her lover,
And master him; he must not be above her.
That is your greatest wish, whether you kill
Or spare me; please yourself. I wait your will."
    In all the court not one that shook her head
190 Or contradicted what the knight had said;
Maid, wife and widow cried, "He's saved his life!"
    And on the word up started the old wife,

---

8. **coverchief. . .caul** kerchief, and a decorative cap, both worn as headgear by
medieval women.

TAKE NOTES

The one the knight saw sitting on the green,
And cried, "Your mercy, sovereign lady queen!
195 Before the court disperses, do me right!
'Twas I who taught this answer to the knight,
For which he swore, and pledged his honor to it,
That the first thing I asked of him he'd do it,
So far as it should lie within his might.
200 Before this court I ask you then, sir knight,
To keep your word and take me for your wife:
For well you know that I have saved your life.
If this be false, deny it on your sword!"
   "Alas!" he said, "Old lady, by the Lord
205 I know indeed that such was my behest,
But for God's love think of a new request,
Take all my goods, but leave my body free."
"A curse on us," she said, "if I agree!
I may be foul, I may be poor and old,
210 Yet will not choose to be, for all the gold
That's bedded in the earth or lies above,
Less than your wife, nay, than your very love!"
   "My love?" said he. "By Heaven, my damnation!
Alas that any of my race and station
215 Should ever make so foul a misalliance!"
Yet in the end his pleading and defiance
All went for nothing, he was forced to wed.
He takes his ancient wife and goes to bed.

   Now peradventure some may well suspect
220 A lack of care in me since I neglect
To tell of the rejoicings and display
Made at the feast upon their wedding-day.
I have but a short answer to let fall;
I say there was no joy or feast at all,
225 Nothing but heaviness of heart and sorrow.
He married her in private on the morrow
And all day long stayed hidden like an owl,
It was such torture that his wife looked foul.
   Great was the anguish churning in his head
230 When he and she were piloted to bed;
He wallowed back and forth in desperate style.
His ancient wife lay smiling all the while;
At last she said, "Bless us! Is this, my dear,
How knights and wives get on together here?

235 Are these the laws of good King Arthur's house?
Are knights of his all so contemptuous?
I am your own beloved and your wife,
And I am she, indeed, that saved your life;
And certainly I never did you wrong.
240 Then why, this first of nights, so sad a song?
You're carrying on as if you were half-witted
Say, for God's love, what sin have I committed?
I'll put things right if you will tell me how."
        "Put right?" he cried. "That never can be now!
245 Nothing can ever be put right again!
You're old, and so abominably plain,
So poor to start with, so low-bred to follow;
It's little wonder if I twist and wallow!
God, that my heart would burst within my breast!"
250   "Is that," said she, "the cause of your unrest?"
        "Yes, certainly," he said, "and can you wonder?"
        "I could set right what you suppose a blunder,
That's if I cared to, in a day or two,
If I were shown more courtesy by you.
255 Just now," she said, "you spoke of gentle birth,
Such as descends from ancient wealth and worth.
If that's the claim you make for gentlemen
Such arrogance is hardly worth a hen.
Whoever loves to work for virtuous ends,
260 Public and private, and who most intends
To do what deeds of gentleness he can,
Take him to be the greatest gentleman.
Christ wills we take our gentleness from Him,
Not from a wealth of ancestry long dim,
265 Though they bequeath their whole establishment
By which we claim to be of high descent.
Our fathers cannot make us a bequest
Of all those virtues that became them best
And earned for them the name of gentleman,
270 But bade us follow them as best we can.
        "Thus the wise poet of the Florentines,
Dante[9] by name, has written in these lines,
For such is the opinion Dante launches:
'Seldom arises by these slender branches
275 prowess of men, for it is God, no less,
Wills us to claim of Him our gentleness.'
For of our parents nothing can we claim

TAKE NOTES

____

____

____

____

____

____

____

____

____

____

____

____

____

____

____

____

____

____

____

____

____

____

____

____

____

____

____

____

____

____

____

Save temporal things, and these may hurt and maim.
   "But everyone knows this as well as I;
280 For if gentility were implanted by
The natural course of lineage down the line,
Public or private, could it cease to shine
In doing the fair work of gentle deed?
No vice or villainy could then bear seed.
285   "Take fire and carry it to the darkest house
Between this kingdom and the Caucasus,[10]
And shut the doors on it and leave it there,
It will burn on, and it will burn as fair
As if ten thousand men were there to see,
290 For fire will keep its nature and degree,
I can assure you, sir, until it dies.
   "But gentleness, as you will recognize,
Is not annexed in nature to possessions,
Men fail in living up to their professions;
295 But fire never ceases to be fire.
God knows you'll often find, if you enquire,
Some lording full of villainy and shame.
If you would be esteemed for the mere name
Of having been by birth a gentleman
300 And stemming from some virtuous, noble clan,
And do not live yourself by gentle deed
Or take your fathers' noble code and creed,
You are no gentleman, though duke or earl.
Vice and bad manners are what make a churl.
305   "Gentility is only the renown
For bounty that your fathers handed down,
Quite foreign to your person, not your own;
Gentility must come from God alone.
That we are gentle comes to us by grace
310 And by no means is it bequeathed with place.
   "Reflect how noble (says Valerius)[11]
Was Tullius surnamed Hostilius,
Who rose from poverty to nobleness.
And read Boethius, Seneca no less,
315 Thus they express themselves and are agreed:
'Gentle is he that does a gentle deed.'
And therefore, my dear husband, I conclude

---

9. **Dante** Dante Alighieri (dän′ tā al əg yer′ ē) (1265–1321) Italian poet who wrote the *Divine Comedy.*
10. **Caucasus** (kô′ kə səs) mountain range between southeastern Europe and western Asia.

That even if my ancestors were rude,
Yet God on high—and so I hope He will—
320 Can grant me grace to live in virtue still,
A gentlewoman only when beginning
To live in virtue and to shrink from sinning.
      "As for my poverty which you reprove,
Almighty God Himself in whom we move,
325 Believe and have our being, chose a life
Of poverty, and every man or wife
Nay, every child can see our Heavenly King
Would never stoop to choose a shameful thing.
No shame in poverty if the heart is gay,
330 As Seneca and all the learned say.
He who accepts his poverty unhurt
I'd say is rich although he lacked a shirt.
But truly poor are they who whine and fret
And covet what they cannot hope to get.
335 And he that, having nothing, covets not,
Is rich, though you may think he is a sot.[12]
      "True poverty can find a song to sing.
Juvenal says a pleasant little thing:
'The poor can dance and sing in the relief
340 Of having nothing that will tempt a thief.'
Though it be hateful, poverty is good,
A great incentive to a livelihood,
And a great help to our capacity
For wisdom, if accepted patiently.
345 Poverty is, though wanting in estate,
A kind of wealth that none calumniate.[13]
Poverty often, when the heart is lowly,
Brings one to God and teaches what is holy,
Gives knowledge of oneself and even lends
350 A glass by which to see one's truest friends.
And since it's no offence, let me be plain;
Do not rebuke my poverty again.
      "Lastly you taxed me, sir, with being old.
Yet even if you never had been told
355 By ancient books, you gentlemen engage
Yourselves in honor to respect old age.

---

11. **Valerius . . . Seneca** Valerius (və lir´ ē əs) Maximus was a first-century a.d. Roman author who collected historical anecdotes. Tullius Hostilius rose from humble beginnings to become a legendary king of Rome. Boethius (bō ē´ thē əs) was a Roman philosopher whose *The Consolation of Philosophy* is a recognized source for Chaucer's writings. Seneca was a Roman philosopher and dramatist.

12. **sot** fool.

13. **calumniate** (kə lum´ ne āt´) slander.

TAKE NOTES

To call an old man 'father' shows good breeding,
And this could be supported from my reading.
   "You say I'm old and fouler than a fen.
360 You need not fear to be a cuckold, then.
Filth and old age, I'm sure you will agree,
Are powerful wardens upon chastity.
Nevertheless, well knowing your delights,
I shall fulfil your worldly appetites.
365   "You have two choices; which one will you try?
To have me old and ugly till I die,
But still a loyal, true and humble wife
That never will displease you all her life,
Or would you rather I were young and pretty
370 And chance your arm what happens in a city
Where friends will visit you because of me,
Yes, and in other places too, maybe.
Which would you have? The choice is all your own."
   The knight thought long, and with a piteous
     groan
375 At last he said, with all the care in life,
"My lady and my love, my dearest wife,
I leave the matter to your wise decision.
You make the choice yourself, for the provision
Of what may be agreeable and rich
380 In honor to us both, I don't care which;
Whatever pleases you suffices me."
   "And have I won the mastery?" said she,
"Since I'm to choose and rule as I think fit?"
"Certainly, wife," he answered her, "that's it."
385 "Kiss me," she cried. "No quarrels! On my oath
And word of honor, you shall find me both,
That is, both fair and faithful as a wife;
May I go howling mad and take my life
Unless I prove to be as good and true
390 As ever wife was since the world was new!
And if to-morrow when the sun's above
I seem less fair than any lady-love,
Than any queen or empress east or west,
Do with my life and death as you think best.
395 Cast up the curtain, husband. Look at me!"
   And when indeed the knight had looked to see,
Lo, she was young and lovely, rich in charms.
In ecstasy he caught her in her arms,

His heart went bathing in a bath of blisses
400 And melted in a hundred thousand kisses,
And she responded in the fullest measure
With all that could delight or give him pleasure.
    So they lived ever after to the end
In perfect bliss; and may Christ Jesus send
405 Us husbands meek and young and fresh in bed,
And grace to overbid them when we wed.
And—Jesu hear my prayer!—cut short the lives
Of those who won't be governed by their wives;
And all old, angry niggards of their pence,[14]
410 God send them soon a very pestilence!

---

14. niggards (nig′ ərdz) **of their pence** misers stingy with their money.

TAKE NOTES

from Morte d'Arthur

by Sir Thomas Malory

This selection begins after King Arthur has traveled to France at the insistence of his nephew, Gawain, to besiege his former friend and knight, Lancelot, for his involvement with Queen Guenevere. However, the king's attempts to punish Lancelot are halfhearted, and he is soon forced to abandon them altogether when he learns that his illegitimate son, Mordred, has seized control of England. Arthur leads his forces back to England, and Mordred attacks them upon their landing. Gawain is killed in the fighting, but before he dies, he manages to send word to Lancelot that Arthur is in need of his assistance.

So upon Trinity Sunday at night King Arthur dreamed a wonderful dream, and in his dream him seemed[1] that he saw upon a chafflet[2] a chair, and the chair was fast to a wheel, and thereupon sat King Arthur in the richest cloth of gold that might be made. And the King thought there was under him, far from him, an hideous deep black water, and therein was all manner of serpents, and worms, and wild beasts, foul and horrible. And suddenly the King thought that the wheel turned upside down, and he fell among the serpents, and every beast took him by a limb. And then the King cried as he lay in his bed, "Help, help!"

And then knights, squires, and yeomen awaked the King, and then he was so amazed that he wist[3] not where he was. And then so he awaked until it was nigh day, and then he fell on slumbering again, not sleeping nor thoroughly waking. So the King seemed[4] verily that there came Sir Gawain unto him with a number of fair ladies with him. So when King Arthur saw him, he said,

---

1. **him seemed** It seemed to him.
2. **chafflet** platform.
3. **wist** knew.
4. **the King seemed** It seemed to the King.

"Welcome, my sister's son. I weened ye had been dead. And now I see thee on-live, much am I beholden unto Almighty Jesu. Ah, fair nephew and my sister's son, what been these ladies that hither be come with you?"

"Sir," said Sir Gawain, "all these be ladies for whom I have foughten for when I was man living. And all these are those that I did battle for in righteous quarrels, and God hath given them that grace, at their great prayer, because I did battle for them for their right, that they should bring me hither unto you. Thus much hath given me leave God, for to warn you of your death. For and ye fight as tomorn[5] with Sir Mordred, as ye both have assigned, doubt ye not ye must be slain, and the most party of your people on both parties. And for the great grace and goodness that Almighty Jesu hath unto you, and for pity of you and many more other good men there shall be slain, God hath sent me to you of his special grace to give you warning that in no wise ye do battle as tomorn, but that ye take a treaty for a month from today. And proffer you largely[6] you so that tomorn ye put in a delay. For within a month shall come Sir Lancelot with all his noble knights and rescue you worshipfully and slay Sir Mordred and all that ever will hold with him."

Then Sir Gawain and all the ladies vanished. And anon the King called upon his knights, squires, and yeomen, and charged them wightly[7] to fetch his noble lords and wise bishops unto him. And when they were come the King told them of his avision,[8] that Sir Gawain had told him and warned him that, and he fought on the morn, he should be slain. Then the King commanded Sir Lucan the Butler and his brother Sir Bedivere the Bold, with two bishops with them, and charged them in any wise to take a treaty for a month from today with Sir Mordred. "And spare not: proffer him lands and goods as much as ye think reasonable."

So then they departed and came to Sir Mordred where he had a grim host of an hundred thousand, and there they entreated Sir Mordred long time. And at the last Sir Mordred was agreed for to have Cornwall

---

5. **and . . . tomorn** "if you fight tomorrow."
6. **proffer you largely** make generous offers.
7. **wightly** quickly.
8. **avision** dream.

TAKE NOTES

and Kent by King Arthur's days, and after that, all England, after the days of King Arthur.

Then were they condescended[9] that King Arthur and Sir Mordred should meet betwixt both their hosts, and each of them should bring fourteen persons. And so they came with this word unto Arthur. Then said he, "I am glad that this is done," and so he went into the field.

And when King Arthur should depart, he warned all his host that, and they see any sword drawn, "Look ye come on fiercely and slay that traitor Sir Mordred, for I in no wise trust him." In like wise Sir Mordred warned his host that "And ye see any manner of sword drawn, look that ye come on fiercely, and so slay all that ever before you standeth, for in no wise I will not trust for this treaty." And in the same wise said Sir Mordred unto his host, "For I know well my father will be avenged upon me."

And so they met as their pointment[10] was and were agreed and accorded thoroughly. And wine was fetched and they drank together. Right so came an adder out of a little heathbush, and it stung a knight in the foot. And so when the knight felt him so stung, he looked down and saw the adder. And anon he drew his sword to slay the adder, and thought none other harm. And when the host on both parties saw that sword drawn, then they blew beams,[11] trumpets, horns, and shouted grimly. And so both hosts dressed them together. And King Arthur took his horse and said, "Alas, this unhappy day!" and so rode to his party, and Sir Mordred in like wise.

And never since was there never seen a more dolefuller battle in no Christian land, for there was but rushing and riding, lunging and striking; and many a grim word was there spoken of either to other, and many a deadly stroke. But ever King Arthur rode throughout the battle[12] of Sir Mordred many times and did full nobly, as a noble king should do, and at all times he fainted never. And Sir Mordred did his devoir[13] that day and put himself in great peril.

---

9. **condescended** agreed.
10. **pointment** arrangement.
11. **beams** type of trumpet.
12. **battle** battalion.
13. **devoir** (də vwär′) *n.* duty (from the French; obsolete).

And thus they fought all the long day, and never stinted[14] till the noble knights were laid to the cold earth. And ever they fought still till it was near night, and by then was there an hundred thousand laid dead upon the down. Then was King Arthur wood-wroth[15] out of measure when he saw his people so slain from him. And so he looked about him and could see no more of all his host, and good knights left no more on-live, but two knights: the t'one was Sir Lucan the Butler and the other his brother Sir Bedivere. And yet they were full sore wounded.

"Jesu, mercy," said the King, "where are all my noble knights become? Alas that ever I should see this doleful day! For now," said King Arthur, "I am come to mine end. But would to God," said he, "that I wist now where were that traitor Sir Mordred that has caused all this mischief."

Then King Arthur looked about and was ware where stood Sir Mordred leaning upon his sword among a great heap of dead men.

"Now give me my spear," said King Arthur unto Sir Lucan, "for yonder I have espied the traitor that all this woe hath wrought."

"Sir, let him be," said Sir Lucan, "for he is unhappy. And if ye pass this unhappy day ye shall be right well revenged upon him. And, good lord, remember ye of your night's dream, and what the spirit of Sir Gawain told you tonight, and yet God of his great goodness hath preserved you hitherto. And for God's sake, my lord, leave off by this, for, blessed be God, ye have won the field: for yet we been here three on-live, and with Sir Mordred is not one on-live. And therefore if ye leave off now, this wicked day of destiny is past."

"Now, tide[16] me death, tide me life," said the King, "now I see him yonder alone, he shall never escape mine hands. For at a better avail shall I never have him."

"God speed you well!" said Sir Bedivere.

Then the King got his spear in both his hands and ran toward Sir Mordred, crying and saying, "Traitor, now is thy deathday come!"

---

14. **stinted** stopped.
15. **wood-wroth** wild with rage.
16. **tide** befall.

TAKE NOTES

And when Sir Mordred saw King Arthur he ran until him with his sword drawn in his hand, and there King Arthur smote Sir Mordred under the shield, with a thrust of his spear, throughout the body more than a fathom. And when Sir Mordred felt that he had his death's wound, he thrust himself with the might that he had up to the burr[17] of King Arthur's spear, and right so he smote his father King Arthur with his sword holden in both his hands, upon the side of the head, that the sword pierced the helmet and the casing of the brain. And therewith Sir Mordred dashed down stark dead to the earth.

And noble King Arthur fell in a swough[18] to the earth, and there he swooned oftentimes, and Sir Lucan and Sir Bedivere ofttimes heaved him up. And so, weakly betwixt them, they led him to a little chapel not far from the seaside, and when the King was there, him thought him reasonably eased. Then heard they people cry in the field. "Now go thou, Sir Lucan," said the King, "and do me to wit[19] what betokens that noise in the field."

So Sir Lucan departed, for he was grievously wounded in many places. And so as he walked he saw and harkened by the moonlight how that pillagers and robbers were come into the field to pill and to rob many a full noble knight of brooches and bracelets and of many a good ring and many a rich jewel. And who that were not dead all out there they slew them for their harness and their riches. When Sir Lucan understood this work, he came to the King as soon as he might and told him all what he had heard and seen. "Therefore by my read,"[20] said Sir Lucan, "it is best that we bring you to some town."

"I would it were so," said the King, "but I may not stand, my head works so. Ah, Sir Lancelot," said King Arthur, "this day have I sore missed thee. And alas that ever I was against thee, for now have I my death, whereof Sir Gawain me warned in my dream."

Then Sir Lucan took up the King the t'one party[21] and Sir Bedivere the other party; and in the lifting up

---

17. **burr** hand guard.
18. **swough** forcible movement
19. **me to wit** "let me know."
20. **read** advice.
21. **party** side.

the King swooned and in the lifting Sir Lucan fell in
a swoon that part of his guts fell out of his body, and
therewith the noble knight's heart burst. And when the
King awoke he beheld Sir Lucan how he lay foaming at
the mouth and part of his guts lay at his feet.

"Alas," said the King, "this is to me a full heavy sight
to see this noble duke so die for my sake, for he would
have helped me that had more need of help than I. Alas
that he would not complain him for his heart was so
set to help me. Now Jesu have mercy upon his soul."

Then Sir Bedivere wept for the death of his brother.

"Now leave this mourning and weeping gentle
knight," said the King, "for all this will not avail me.
For wit thou well, and might I live myself, the death
of Sir Lucan would grieve me evermore. But my time
passeth on fast," said the King. "Therefore," said King
Arthur unto Sir Bedivere, "take thou here Excalibur my
good sword and go with it to yonder water's side; and
when thou comest there I charge thee throw my sword
in that water and come again and tell me what thou
sawest there."

"My lord," said Sir Bedivere, "your commandment
shall be done, and I shall lightly[22] bring you word
again."

So Sir Bedivere departed. And by the way he beheld
that noble sword, that the pommel and the haft[23] was
all precious stones. And then he said to himself, "If I
throw this rich sword in the water, thereof shall never
come good, but harm and loss." And then Sir Bedivere
hid Excalibur under a tree. And so, as soon as he
might, he came again unto the King and said he had
been at the water and had thrown the sword into the
water.

"What saw thou there?" said the King.

"Sir," he said, "I saw nothing but waves and winds."

"That is untruly said of thee," said the King.
"And therefore go thou lightly again and do my
commandment; as thou art to me loved and dear,
spare not, but throw it in."

Then Sir Bedivere returned again and took the sword
in his hand. And yet him thought sin and shame to

---

22. lightly quickly.
23. pommel . . . haft hilt and hand guard.

TAKE NOTES

throw away that noble sword. And so eft[24] he hid the sword and returned again and told the King that he had been at the water and done his commandment.

"What sawest thou there?" said the King.

"Sir," he said, "I saw nothing but waters wap and waves wan."[25]

"Ah, traitor unto me and untrue," said King Arthur, "now hast thou betrayed me twice. Who would have weened that thou that has been to me so loved and dear, and thou art named a noble knight, and would betray me for the riches of this sword. But now go again lightly, for thy long tarrying putteth me in great jeopardy of my life, for I have taken cold. And but if thou do now as I bid thee, if ever I may see thee I shall slay thee mine own hands, for thou wouldest for my rich sword see me dead."

Then Sir Bedivere departed and went to the sword and lightly took it up, and so he went to the water's side; and there he bound the girdle about the hilts, and threw the sword as far into the water as he might. And there came an arm and an hand above the water and took it and clutched it, and shook it thrice and brandished; and then vanished away the hand with the sword into the water. So Sir Bedivere came again to the King and told him what he saw.

"Alas," said the King, "help me hence, for I dread me I have tarried overlong."

Then Sir Bedivere took the King upon his back and so went with him to that water's side. And when they were at the water's side, even fast[26] by the bank floated a little barge with many fair ladies in it; and among them all was a queen; and all they had black hoods, and all they wept and shrieked when they saw King Arthur.

"Now put me into that barge," said the King; and so he did softly. And there received him three ladies with great mourning, and so they set them down. And in one of their laps King Arthur laid his head, and then the queen said, "Ah, my dear brother, why have ye tarried so long from me? Alas, this wound on your head hath caught overmuch cold." And anon they

---

24. **eft** again.
25. **waters . . . wan** waters lap and waves grow dark.
26. **fast** close.

rowed fromward the land, and Sir Bedivere beheld all those ladies go froward him.

Then Sir Bedivere cried and said, "Ah, my lord Arthur, what shall become of me, now ye go from me and leave me here alone among mine enemies?"

"Comfort thyself," said the King, "and do as well as thou mayest, for in me is no trust for to trust in. For I must into the vale of Avilion[27] to heal me of my grievous wound. And if thou hear nevermore of me, pray for my soul."

But ever the queen and ladies wept and shrieked, that it was pity to hear. And as soon as Sir Bedivere had lost sight of the barge he wept and wailed, and so took the forest and went all that night.

And in the morning he was ware, betwixt two bare woods, of a chapel and an hermitage. Then was Sir Bedivere glad, and thither he went, and when he came into the chapel he saw where lay an hermit groveling on all fours, close thereby a tomb was new dug. When the hermit saw Sir Bedivere he knew him well, for he was but little tofore Bishop of Canterbury, that Sir Mordred put to flight.

"Sirs," said Sir Bedivere, "what man is there here interred that you pray so fast for?"

"Fair son," said the hermit. "I wot not verily but by guessing. But this same night, at midnight, here came a number of ladies and brought here a dead corpse and prayed me to inter him. And here they offered an hundred tapers, and gave me a thousand gold coins."

"Alas," said Sir Bedivere, "that was my lord King Arthur, which lieth here buried in this chapel."

Then Sir Bedivere swooned, and when he awoke he prayed the hermit that he might abide with him still, there to live with fasting and prayers:

"For from hence will I never go," said Sir Bedivere, "by my will, but all the days of my life here to pray for my lord Arthur."

"Sir, ye are welcome to me," said the hermit, "for I know you better than ye think that I do: for ye are Sir Bedivere the Bold, and the full noble duke Sir Lucan the Butler was your brother."

Then Sir Bedivere told the hermit all as you have heard tofore, and so he stayed with the hermit that

---

27. **Avilion** legendary island where Arthur is said to dwell until his return.

TAKE NOTES

was beforehand Bishop of Canterbury. And there Sir Bedivere put upon him poor clothes, and served the hermit full lowly in fasting and in prayers.

Thus of Arthur I find no more written in books that been authorized, neither more of the very certainty of his death heard I nor read, but thus was he led away in a ship wherein were three queens; that one was King Arthur's sister, Queen Morgan le Fay, the other was the Queen of North Galis, and the third was the Queen of the Waste Lands.

Now more of the death of King Arthur could I never find, but that these ladies brought him to his grave, and such one was interred there which the hermit bare witness that was once Bishop of Canterbury. But yet the hermit knew not in certain that he was verily the body of King Arthur; for this tale Sir Bedivere, a knight of the Table Round, made it to be written.

Yet some men say in many parts of England that King Arthur is not dead, but carried by the will of our Lord Jesu into another place; and men say that he shall come again, and he shall win the Holy Cross. Yet I will not say that it shall be so, but rather I would say: here in this world he changed his life. And many men say that there is written upon the tomb this:

HIC IACET ARTHURUS, REX QUONDAM, REXQUE FUTURUS[28]

---

28. HIC . . . FUTURUS Here lies Arthur, who was once king and king will be again.

Sonnet 1

by Edmund Spenser

Happy ye leaves when as those lily hands,
Which hold my life in their dead doing[1] might,
Shall handle you and hold in love's soft bands,
Like captives trembling at the victor's sight,
5 And happy lines, on which with starry light,
Those lamping[2] eyes will deign sometimes to look
And read the sorrows of my dying spright,[3]
Written with tears in heart's close[4] bleeding book.
And happy rhymes bathed in the sacred brook
10 Of Helicon[5] whence she derived is,
When ye behold that angel's blessed look,
My soul's long lacked food, my heaven's bliss.
Leaves, lines, and rhymes, seek her to please alone,
Whom if ye please, I care for other none.

---

1. **doing** killing.
2. **lamping** flashing.
3. **spright** spirit.
4. **close** secret.
5. **Helicon** In Greek mythology, the mountain home of the Muses, goddesses of the arts.

TAKE NOTES

TAKE NOTES

Sonnet 35

by Edmund Spenser

My hungry eyes through greedy covetize,[1]
Still[2] to behold the object of their pain,
With no contentment can themselves suffice:
But having pine[3] and having not complain.
5 For lacking it they cannot life sustain,
And having it they gaze on it the more:
In their amazement like Narcissus[4] vain
Whose eyes him starved: so plenty makes me poor.
Yet are mine eyes so fillèd with the store
10 Of that fair sight, that nothing else they brook,
But loathe the things which they did like before,
And can no more endure on them to look.
All this world's glory seemeth vain to me,
And all their shows but shadows, saving she.

---

1. **covetize** *v.* desire excessively.
2. **Still** *adv.* always.
3. **pine** *v.* yearn.
4. **Narcissus** in Greek mythology, a youth who fell in love with his own reflection in a pool, wasted away with yearning, and was changed after his death into the narcissus flower.

Sonnet 75

by Edmund Spenser

One day I wrote her name upon the strand,[1]
But came the waves and washèd it away:
Again I wrote it with a second hand,
But came the tide, and made my pains his prey.
5 "Vain man," said she, "that dost in vain assay,
A mortal thing so to immortalize,
For I myself shall like to this decay,
And eek[2] my name be wipèd out likewise."
"Not so," quod[3] I, "let baser things devise
10 To die in dust, but you shall live by fame:
My verse your virtues rare shall eternize,
And in the heavens write your glorious name.
Where whenas death shall all the world subdue,
Our love shall live, and later life renew."

---

1. **strand** beach.
2. **eek** also.
3. **quod** said.

TAKE NOTES

Speech Before Her Troops

by Queen Elizabeth I

BACKGROUND *By the 1580s, Philip II was king of Portugal as well as Spain and ruled over vast New World colonies. He also ruled the Spanish Netherlands (today's Netherlands and some adjoining areas), where his repression of Protestants prompted the Dutch to rebel. Philip's Protestant half-sister-in-law, Elizabeth I, queen of England, aided the Dutch rebels and quietly supported attacks on Spanish ships by English sea captains. In 1587, when a plot to replace her with her Catholic cousin Mary, Queen of Scots, ended in failure, Elizabeth had Mary executed. A year later, Philip sent his Armada of warships to collect troops fighting in the Netherlands and invade England.*

With Elizabeth's navy fighting the Spanish fleet, her land forces massed in the English port of Tilbury, anticipating an invasion that never came. Nerves frayed and soldiers began to grumble about delays in pay. Then Elizabeth, dramatically dressed in a white gown and silver breast-plate, appeared before the troops and made the following famous speech.

My loving people, we have been persuaded by some, that are careful of our safety, to take heed how we commit ourselves to armed multitudes,[1] for fear of treachery: but I assure you, I do not desire to live to distrust my faithful and loving people. Let tyrants fear; I have always so behaved myself that, under God, I have placed my chiefest strength and safeguard in the loyal hearts and good will of my subjects. And therefore I am come amongst you at this time, not as for my recreation or sport, but being resolved, in the midst and heat of the battle, to live or die amongst you all; to lay down, for my God, and for my kingdom, and for my people, my honor and my blood, even the dust. I know I have but the body of a weak and feeble woman; but

---

1. **armed multitudes** troops with weapons, like those she is addressing.

I have the heart of a king, and of a king of England, too; and think foul scorn that Parma[2] or Spain, or any prince of Europe, should dare to invade the borders of my realms: to which, rather than any dishonor should grow by me, I myself will take up arms; I myself will be your general, judge, and rewarder of every one of your virtues in the field. I know already, by your forwardness, that you have deserved rewards and crowns;[3] and we do assure you, on the word of a prince, they shall be duly paid you. In the mean my lieutenant general shall be in my stead, than whom never prince commanded a more noble and worthy subject; not doubting by your obedience to my general, by your concord in the camp, and by your valor in the field, we shall shortly have a famous victory over the enemies of my God, of my kingdom, and of my people.

---

2. **Parma** Alessandro Farnese (1545–1592), duke of the Italian state of Parma and commander of Philip II's troops fighting rebels in the Spanish Netherlands.
3. **crowns** coins depicting the monarch's head, used to pay the troops.

TAKE NOTES

The Tragedy of Macbeth, Act I

by William Shakespeare

BACKGROUND *The Elizabethans viewed the universe, in its ideal state, as both orderly and interconnected. They believed that a great chain linked all beings, from God on high to the lowest beasts and plants. They also believed that universal order was based on parallels between different realms. Just as the sun ruled in the heavens, for example, the king ruled in the state and the father in the family. Because everything was linked, a disturbance in one area would cause a disturbance in others. In keeping with this concept of order, a Shakespearean tragedy shows how a tragic hero's bad choices can disturb the whole universe. As Macbeth gets under way, notice the parallel disorders in the mind of the hero, the weather, and the kingdom.*

DUNCAN, King of Scotland

MALCOLM
DONALBAIN } his sons

MACBETH
BANQUO
MACDUFF
LENNOX
ROSS } noblemen of Scotland
MENTEITH
ANGUS
CAITHNESS

FLEANCE, son to Banquo
SIWARD, Earl of Northumberland, general of the English forces
YOUNG SIWARD, his son

SEYTON, an officer attending on Macbeth
SON TO MACDUFF
AN ENGLISH DOCTOR
A SCOTTISH DOCTOR
A PORTER
AN OLD MAN
THREE MURDERERS
LADY MACBETH
LADY MACDUFF
A GENTLEWOMAN attending on Lady Macbeth
HECATE
WITCHES
APPARITIONS
LORDS, OFFICERS, SOLDIERS, ATTENDANTS, AND MESSENGERS

Setting: Scotland; England

Act I

Scene i. An open place.

[*Thunder and lightning. Enter* THREE WITCHES.]

FIRST WITCH. When shall we three meet again?
  In thunder, lightning, or in rain?

SECOND WITCH. When the hurlyburly's done,
  When the battle's lost and won.

5 **THIRD WITCH.** That will be ere the set of sun.

FIRST WITCH. Where the place?

SECOND WITCH.   Upon the heath.

THIRD WITCH. There to meet with Macbeth.

FIRST WITCH. I come, Graymalkin.[1]

SECOND WITCH. Paddock[2] calls.

THIRD WITCH.   Anon![3]

10 **ALL.** Fair is foul, and foul is fair.

  Hover through the fog and filthy air.   [*Exit.*]

Scene ii. A camp near Forres, a town in northeast Scotland.

[*ALARUM WITHIN.[1] Enter* KING DUNCAN, MALCOLM, DONALBAIN, LENNOX, *with* ATTENDANTS, *meeting a bleeding* CAPTAIN.]

KING. What bloody man is that? He can report,
  As seemeth by his plight, of the revolt
  The newest state.

MALCOLM.   This is the sergeant[2]
  Who like a good and hardy soldier fought
5 'Gainst my captivity. Hail, brave friend!
  Say to the king the knowledge of the broil[3]
  As thou didst leave it.

---

1. **Graymalkin** first witch's helper, a gray cat.
2. **Paddock** second witch's helper, a toad.
3. **Anon** at once.

---

1. **Alarum within** trumpet call offstage.
2. **sergeant** officer.
3. **broil** battle.

TAKE NOTES

____

CAPTAIN.   Doubtful it stood,
As two spent swimmers, that do cling together
And choke their art.[4] The merciless Macdonwald—
10 Worthy to be a rebel for to that
The multiplying villainies of nature
Do swarm upon him—from the Western Isles[5]
Of kerns and gallowglasses[6] is supplied;
And fortune, on his damnéd quarrel[7] smiling,
15 Showed like a rebel's whore:[8] but all's too weak:
For brave Macbeth—well he deserves that
          name—
Disdaining fortune, with his brandished steel,
Which smoked with bloody execution,
Like valor's minion[9] carved out his passage
20 Till he faced the slave;
Which nev'r shook hands, nor bade farewell to
          him,
Till he unseamed him from the nave to th' chops,[10]
And fixed his head upon our battlements.

KING. O valiant cousin! Worthy gentleman!

25 **CAPTAIN.** As whence the sun 'gins his reflection[11]
Shipwracking storms and direful thunders break,
So from that spring whence comfort seemed to
          come
Discomfort swells. Mark, King of Scotland, mark:
No sooner justice had, with valor armed,
30 Compelled these skipping kerns to trust their
heels
But the Norweyan lord,[12] surveying vantage,[13]
With furbished arms and new supplies of men,
Began a fresh assault.

KING.   Dismayed not this
Our captains, Macbeth and Banquo?

CAPTAIN.   Yes;
35 As sparrows eagles, or the hare the lion.

---

4. **choke their art** prevent each other from swimming.
5. **Western Isles** the Hebrides, off Scotland.
6. **Of kerns and gallow-glasses** with lightly armed Irish foot soldiers and heavily armed soldiers.
7. **damned quarrel** accursed cause.
8. **Showed . . . whore** falsely appeared to favor Macdonwald.
9. **minion** favorite.
10. **unseamed . . . chops** split him open from the navel to the jaws.
11. **gins his reflection** rises.
12. **Norweyan lord** king of Norway.
13. **surveying vantage** seeing an opportunity.

If I say sooth,[14] I must report they were
As cannons overcharged with double cracks;[15]
So they doubly redoubled strokes upon the foe.
Except[16] they meant to bathe in reeking wounds,
40   Or memorize another Golgotha,[17]
I cannot tell—
But I am faint; my gashes cry for help.
  KING. So well thy words become thee as thy wounds;
They smack of honor both. Go get him surgeons.

[*Exit* CAPTAIN, *attended.*]

[*Enter* ROSS *and* ANGUS.]

Who comes here?

45   **MALCOLM.**   The worthy Thane[18] of Ross.

  LENNOX. What a haste looks through his eyes! So
    should he look
That seems to[19] speak things strange.

  ROSS.   God save the king!

  KING. Whence cam'st thou, worthy Thane?

  ROSS.   From Fife, great King;
Where the Norweyan banners flout the sky
50   And fan our people cold.
Norway[20] himself, with terrible numbers,
Assisted by that most disloyal traitor
The Thane of Cawdor, began a dismal[21] conflict;
Till that Bellona's bridegroom, lapped in proof,[22]
55   Confronted him with self-comparisons,[23]
Point against point, rebellious arm 'gainst arm,
Curbing his lavish[24] spirit: and, to conclude,
The victory fell on us.

---

14. sooth truth.
15. cracks explosives.
16. except unless.
17. memorize . . . Golgotha (gôl′ gə thə) make the place as memorable for
    slaughter as Golgotha, the place where Christ was crucified.
18. Thane Scottish title of nobility.
19. seems to seems about to.
20. Norway king of Norway.
21. dismal threatening.
22. Bellona's . . . proof Macbeth is called the mate of Bellona, the goddess of war,
    clad in tested armor.
23. self-comparisons counter movements.
24. lavish insolent.

TAKE NOTES

____

____

____

____

____

____

____

____

____

____

____

____

____

____

____

____

____

____

____

____

____

____

____

____

____

KING.   Great happiness!

ROSS.   That now
   Sweno, the Norways' king, craves composition;[25]
60   Nor would we deign him burial of his men
   Till he disbursed, at Saint Colme's Inch,[26]
   Ten thousand dollars to our general use.

KING. No more that Thane of Cawdor shall deceive
   Our bosom interest:[27] go pronounce his present[28]
      death,
65   And with his former title greet Macbeth.

ROSS. I'll see it done.

KING. What he hath lost, noble Macbeth hath won.

                                    [*Exit.*]

Scene iii. A heath near Forres.

[*Thunder. Enter the* THREE WITCHES.]

FIRST WITCH. Where hast thou been, sister?

SECOND WITCH. Killing swine.[1]

THIRD WITCH. Sister, where thou?

FIRST WITCH. A sailor's wife had chestnuts in her lap,
   And mounched, and mounched, and mounched.
5   "Give me," quoth I.
   "Aroint thee,[2] witch!" the rump-fed ronyon[3] cries.
   Her husband's to Aleppo[4] gone, master o' th' Tiger:
   But in a sieve[5] I'll thither sail,
   And, like a rat without a tail,[6]
10   I'll do, I'll do, and I'll do.

SECOND WITCH. I'll give thee a wind.

FIRST WITCH. Th' art kind.

THIRD WITCH. And I another.

FIRST WITCH. I myself have all the other;

---

25. **composition** terms of peace.
26. **St. Colme's Inch** island near Edinburgh, Scotland.
27. **our bosom interest** my heart's trust.
28. **present** immediate.

---

1. **Killing swine** It was commonly believed that witches killed domestic animals.
2. **Aroint thee** Be off.
3. **rump-fed ronyon** fat-rumped, scabby creature.
4. **Aleppo** trading center in Syria.
5. **sieve** It was commonly believed that witches often sailed in sieves.
6. **rat . . . tail** According to popular belief, witches could assume the form of any animal, but the tail would always be missing.

15 And the very ports they blow,[7]
All the quarters that they know
I' th' shipman's card.[8]
I'll drain him dry as hay:
Sleep shall neither night nor day
20 Hang upon his penthouse lid;[9]
He shall live a man forbid:[10]
Weary sev'nights[11] nine times nine
Shall he dwindle, peak,[12] and pine:
Though his bark cannot be lost,
25 Yet it shall be tempest-tossed.
Look what I have.

SECOND WITCH. Show me, show me.

FIRST WITCH. Here I have a pilot's thumb,
Wracked as homeward he did come.

[*Drum within.*]

30 **THIRD WITCH.** A drum, a drum!
Macbeth doth come.

ALL. The weird[13] sisters, hand in hand,
Posters[14] of the sea and land,
Thus do go about, about:
35 Thrice to thine, and thrice to mine,
And thrice again, to make up nine.
Peace! The charm's wound up.

[*Enter* MACBETH *and* BANQUO.]

MACBETH. So foul and fair a day I have not seen.

BANQUO. How far is 't called to Forres? What are these
40 So withered, and so wild in their attire,
That look not like th' inhabitants o' th' earth,
And yet are on 't? Live you, or are you aught
That man may question? You seem to under-
    stand me,
By each at once her choppy[15] finger laying

---

7. **they blow** to which the winds blow.
8. **card** compass.
9. **penthouse lid** eyelid.
10. **forbid** cursed.
11. **sev'nights** weeks.
12. **peak** waste away.
13. **weird** destiny-serving.
14. **Posters** swift travelers.
15. **choppy** chapped.

TAKE NOTES

____
____
____
____
____
____
____
____
____
____
____
____
____
____
____
____
____
____
____
____
____
____
____
____
____
____
____

45   Upon her skinny lips. You should be women,
And yet your beards forbid me to interpret
That you are so.

MACBETH.   Speak, if you can: what are you?

FIRST WITCH. All hail, Macbeth! Hail to thee, Thane
   of Glamis!

SECOND WITCH. All hail, Macbeth! Hail to thee, Thane
   of Cawdor!

50 **THIRD WITCH.** All hail, Macbeth, that shalt be King
   hereafter!

BANQUO. Good sir, why do you start, and seem to fear
   Things that do sound so fair? I' th' name of truth,
   Are you fantastical,[16] or that indeed
   Which outwardly ye show? My noble partner
55   You greet with present grace[17] and great prediction
   Of noble having[18] and of royal hope,
   That he seems rapt withal:[19] to me you speak not.
   If you can look into the seeds of time,
   And say which grain will grow and which will not,
60   Speak then to me, who neither beg nor fear
   Your favors nor your hate.

FIRST WITCH. Hail!

SECOND WITCH. Hail!

THIRD WITCH. Hail!

65 **FIRST WITCH.** Lesser than Macbeth, and greater.

SECOND WITCH. Not so happy,[20] yet much happier.

THIRD WITCH. Thou shalt get kings, though thou be
   none.
   So all hail, Macbeth and Banquo!
FIRST WITCH. Banquo and Macbeth, all hail!

70 **MACBETH.** Stay, you imperfect[21] speakers, tell me more:
   By Sinel's[22] death I know I am Thane of Glamis;
   But how of Cawdor? The Thane of Cawdor lives,
   A prosperous gentleman; and to be King
   Stands not within the prospect of belief,

---

16. fantastical imaginary.
17. grace honor.
18. having possession.
19. rapt withal entranced by it.
20. happy fortunate.
21. imperfect incomplete.
22. Sinel's (sī′ nəlz) Macbeth's father's.

75 No more than to be Cawdor. Say from whence
You owe[23] this strange intelligence?[24] Or why
Upon this blasted heath you stop our way
With such prophetic greeting? Speak, I charge you.

[WITCHES *vanish.*]

BANQUO. The earth hath bubbles as the water has,
80 And these are of them. Whither are they vanished?

MACBETH. Into the air, and what seemed corporal[25]
melted
As breath into the wind. Would they had stayed!

BANQUO. Were such things here as we do speak
about?
Or have we eaten on the insane root[26]
85 That takes the reason prisoner?

MACBETH. Your children shall be kings.

BANQUO.   You shall be King.

MACBETH. And Thane of Cawdor too. Went it not so?

BANQUO. To th' selfsame tune and words. Who's
here?

[*Enter* ROSS *and* ANGUS.]

ROSS. The King hath happily received, Macbeth,
90 The news of thy success; and when he reads[27]
Thy personal venture in the rebels' fight,
His wonders and his praises do contend
Which should be thine or his.[28] Silenced with that,
In viewing o'er the rest o' th' selfsame day,
95 He finds thee in the stout Norweyan ranks,
Nothing afeard of what thyself didst make,
Strange images of death.[29] As thick as tale
Came post with post,[30] and every one did bear
Thy praises in his kingdom's great defense,
And poured them down before him.

---

23. **owe** own.
24. **intelligence** information.
25. **corporal** real.
26. **insane root** henbane or hemlock, believed to cause insanity.
27. **reads** considers.
28. **His wonders . . . his** His admiration contends with his desire to praise you.
29. **Nothing . . . death** killing, but not being afraid of being killed.
30. **As thick . . . post** as fast as could be counted came messenger after
messenger.

TAKE NOTES

TAKE NOTES

100 **ANGUS.**   We are sent
To give thee, from our royal master, thanks;
Only to herald thee into his sight,
Not pay thee.

ROSS. And for an earnest[31] of a greater honor,
105 He bade me, from him, call thee Thane of Cawdor;
In which addition,[32] hail, most worthy Thane!
For it is thine.

BANQUO. [*Aside*] What, can the devil speak true?

MACBETH. The Thane of Cawdor lives: why do you dress me
In borrowed robes?

ANGUS.   Who was the thane lives yet,
110 But under heavy judgment bears that life
Which he deserves to lose. Whether he was combined[33]
With those of Norway, or did line[34] the rebel
With hidden help and vantage,[35] or that with both
He labored in his country's wrack,[36] I know not;
115 But **treasons** capital, confessed and proved,
Have overthrown him.

MACBETH.   [*Aside*] Glamis, and Thane of Cawdor:
The greatest is behind.[37] [*To* ROSS *and* ANGUS]
Thanks for your pains.
[*Aside to* BANQUO] Do you not hope your children shall be kings,
When those that gave the Thane of Cawdor to me
Promised no less to them?

120 **BANQUO.** [*Aside to* MACBETH] That, trusted home,[38]
Might yet enkindle you unto[39] the crown,
Besides the Thane of Cawdor. But 'tis strange:
And oftentimes, to win us to our harm,
The instruments of darkness tell us truths,

---

31. earnest pledge.
32. In which addition with this new title.
33. combined allied.
34. line support.
35. vantage assistance.
36. wrack ruin.
37. behind still to come.
38. home fully.
39. enkindle you unto encourage you to hope for.

125 Win us with honest trifles, to betray 's
In deepest consequence.
Cousins,⁴⁰ a word, I pray you.

MACBETH.   [Aside] Two truths are told,
As happy prologues to the swelling act
Of the imperial theme.⁴¹—I thank you, gentlemen.—
130 [*Aside*] This supernatural soliciting
Cannot be ill, cannot be good. If ill,
Why hath it given me earnest of success,
Commencing in a truth? I am Thane of Cawdor:
If good, why do I yield to that suggestion⁴²
135 Whose horrid image doth unfix my hair
And make my seated⁴³ heart knock at my ribs,
Against the use of nature?⁴⁴ Present fears
Are less than horrible imaginings.
My thought, whose murder yet is but fantastical
140 Shakes so my single⁴⁵ state of man that function
Is smothered in surmise, and nothing is
But what is not.

BANQUO.   Look, how our partner's rapt.

MACBETH. [*Aside*] If chance will have me King, why,
    chance may crown me,
Without my stir.

BANQUO.   New honors come upon him,
145 Like our strange⁴⁶ garments, cleave not to their
    mold
But with the aid of use.

MACBETH.   [*Aside*] Come what come may,
Time and the hour runs through the roughest day.

BANQUO. Worthy Macbeth, we stay upon your leisure.⁴⁷

MACBETH. Give me your favor.⁴⁸ My dull brain was
    wrought
150 With things forgotten. Kind gentlemen, your pains
Are registered where every day I turn
The leaf to read them. Let us toward the King.

---

40. **Cousins** often used as a term of courtesy between fellow noblemen.
41. **swelling . . . theme** stately idea that I will be King.
42. **suggestion** thought of murdering Duncan.
43. **seated** fixed.
44. **Against . . . nature** in an unnatural way.
45. **single** unaided, weak.
46. **strange** new.
47. **stay upon your leisure** await your convenience.
48. **favor** pardon.

TAKE NOTES

____

[*Aside to* BANQUO] Think upon what hath chanced,
   and at more time,
The interim having weighed it,[49] let us speak
Our free hearts[50] each to other.

155 **BANQUO.**   Very gladly.

MACBETH. Till then, enough. Come, friends.

                    [*Exit.*]

Scene iv. Forres. The palace.

[*Flourish.*[1] *Enter* KING DUNCAN, LENNOX, MALCOLM, DONALBAIN, *and* ATTENDANTS.]

KING. Is execution done on Cawdor? Are not
Those in commission[2] yet returned?

MALCOLM.   My liege,[3]
They are not yet come back. But I have spoke
With one that saw him die, who did report
5   That very frankly he confessed his treasons,
Implored your Highness' pardon and set forth
A deep repentance: nothing in his life
Became him like the leaving it. He died
As one that had been studied[4] in his death,
10   To throw away the dearest thing he owed[5]
As 'twere a careless[6] trifle.

KING.   There's no art
To find the mind's construction[7] in the face:
He was a gentleman on whom I built
An absolute trust.

[*Enter* MACBETH, BANQUO, ROSS, *and* ANGUS.]

             O worthiest cousin!
15   The sin of my ingratitude even now
Was heavy on me: thou art so far before,
That swiftest wing of recompense is slow
To overtake thee. Would thou hadst less deserved,
That the proportion both of thanks and payment

---

49. The interim . . . it when we have had time to think about it.
50. Our free hearts our minds freely.

---

1. Flourish trumpet fanfare.
2. in commission commissioned to oversee the execution.
3. liege (lèj) *n.* lord or king.
4. studied rehearsed.
5. owed owned.
6. careless worthless.
7. mind's construction person's character.

20   Might have been mine!⁸ Only I have left to say,
     More is thy due than more than all can pay.

     MACBETH. The service and the loyalty I owe,
     In doing it, pays itself.⁹ Your Highness' part
     Is to receive our duties: and our duties
25   Are to your throne and state children and servants;
     Which do but what they should, by doing every
        thing
     Safe toward¹⁰ your love and honor.

     KING.   Welcome hither.
     I have begun to plant thee, and will labor
     To make thee full of growing. Noble Banquo,
30   That hast no less deserved, nor must be known
     No less to have done so, let me enfold thee
     And hold thee to my heart.

     BANQUO.   There if I grow,
     The harvest is your own.

     KING.   My plenteous joys,
     Wanton¹¹ in fullness, seek to hide themselves
35   In drops of sorrow. Sons, kinsmen, thanes,
     And you whose places are the nearest, know,
     We will establish our estate upon
     Our eldest, Malcolm,¹² whom we name hereafter
     The Prince of Cumberland: which honor must
40   Not unaccompanied invest him only,
     But signs of nobleness, like stars, shall shine
     On all deservers. From hence to Inverness,¹³
     And bind us further to you.

     MACBETH. The rest is labor, which is not used for you.¹⁴
45   I'll be myself the harbinger,¹⁵ and make joyful
     The hearing of my wife with your approach;
     So, humbly take my leave.

---

8. **Would . . . mine** If you had been less worthy, my thanks and payment could
   have exceeded the rewards you deserve.
9. **pays itself** is its own reward.
10. **Safe toward** with sure regard for.
11. **Wanton** unrestrained.
12. **establish . . . Malcolm** make Malcolm the heir to my throne.
13. **Inverness** Macbeth's castle.
14. **The rest . . . you** anything not done for you is laborious.
15. **harbinger** advance representative of the army or royal party who makes
    arrangements for a visit.

TAKE NOTES

TAKE NOTES

KING. My worthy Cawdor!

MACBETH. [*Aside*] The Prince of Cumberland! That is a step
On which I must fall down, or else o'erleap,
50 For in my way it lies. Stars, hide your fires;
Let not light see my black and deep desires:
The eye wink at the hand;[16] yet let that be
Which the eye fears, when it is done, to see.

[*Exit.*]

KING. True, worthy Banquo; he is full so valiant,
55 And in his commendations I am fed;
It is a banquet to me. Let's after him,
Whose care is gone before to bid us welcome.
It is a peerless kinsman.   [*Flourish. Exit.*]

Scene v. Inverness. Macbeth's castle.

[*Enter* MACBETH'S WIFE, *alone, with a letter.*]

LADY MACBETH. [*Reads*] "They met me in the day of
success; and I have learned by the perfect'st report
they have more in them than mortal knowledge.
When I burned in desire to question them further,
they made themselves air, into which they
vanished.
5 Whiles I stood rapt in the wonder of it, came
missives[1] from the King, who all-hailed me 'Thane
of Cawdor'; by which title, before, these weird sisters
saluted me, and referred me to the coming on
of time, with 'Hail, King that shalt be!' This have I
10 thought good to deliver thee,[2] my dearest partner of
greatness, that thou mightst not lose the dues of
rejoicing, by being ignorant of what greatness is
promised thee. Lay it to thy heart, and farewell."

15 Glamis thou art, and Cawdor, and shalt be
What thou art promised. Yet do I fear thy nature;
It is too full o' th' milk of human kindness
To catch the nearest[3] way. Thou wouldst be great,
Art not without ambition, but without

---

16. **wink at the hand** be blind to the hand's deed.

---

1. **missives** messengers.
2. **deliver thee** report to you.
3. **nearest** quickest.

20 The illness[4] should attend it. What thou wouldst
        highly,
   That wouldst thou holily; wouldst not play false,
   And yet wouldst wrongly win. Thou'dst have,
        great Glamis,
   That which cries "Thus thou must do" if thou
        have it;
   And that which rather thou dost fear to do
25 Than wishest should be undone.[5] Hie thee hither,
   That I may pour my spirits in thine ear,
   And chastise with the valor of my tongue
   All that impedes thee from the golden round[6]
   Which fate and metaphysical aid doth seem
   To have thee crowned withal.

[*Enter* MESSENGER.]
30   What is your tidings?

   MESSENGER. The King comes here tonight.

   LADY MACBETH.   Thou'rt mad to say it!
   Is not thy master with him, who, were't so,
   Would have informed for preparation?

   MESSENGER. So please you, it is true. Our thane is
        coming.
35 One of my fellows had the speed of him,[7]
   Who, almost dead for breath, had scarcely more
   Than would make up his message.

   LADY MACBETH.   Give him tending;
   He brings great news.   [*Exit* MESSENGER.]
                          The raven himself is hoarse
   That croaks the fatal entrance of Duncan
40 Under my battlements. Come, you spirits
   That tend on mortal[8] thoughts, unsex me here,
   And fill me, from the crown to the toe, top-full
   Of direst cruelty! Make thick my blood,
   Stop up th' access and passage to remorse[9]

---

4. illness wickedness.
5. that which . . . undone What you are afraid of doing you would not wish
undone once you have done it.
6. round crown.
7. had . . . him overtook him.
8. mortal deadly.
9. remorse compassion.

TAKE NOTES

45 That no compunctious visitings of nature[10]
Shake my fell[11] purpose, nor keep peace between
Th' effect[12] and it! Come to my woman's breasts,
And take my milk for gall,[13] you murd'ring
     ministers,[14]
Wherever in your sightless[15] substances
50 You wait on[16] nature's mischief! Come, thick night,
And pall[17] thee in the dunnest[18] smoke of hell,
That my keen knife see not the wound it makes,
Nor heaven peep through the blanket of the dark,
To cry "Hold, hold!"

[*Enter* MACBETH.]

                              Great Glamis! Worthy Cawdor!
55 Greater than both, by the all-hail hereafter!
Thy letters have transported me beyond
This ignorant[19] present, and I feel now
The future in the instant.[20]

MACBETH.   My dearest love,
Duncan comes here tonight.

LADY MACBETH.   And when goes hence?

MACBETH. Tomorrow, as he purposes.

60 **LADY MACBETH.**   O, never
Shall sun that morrow see!
Your face, my Thane, is as a book where men
May read strange matters. To beguile the time,[21]
Look like the time; bear welcome in your eye,
65 Your hand, your tongue: look like th' innocent
     flower,
But be the serpent under 't. He that's coming
Must be provided for: and you shall put
This night's great business into my dispatch;[22]
Which shall to all our nights and days to come

---

10. **compunctious . . . nature** natural feelings of pity.
11. **fell** savage.
12. **effect** fulfillment.
13. **milk for gall** kindness in exchange for bitterness.
14. **ministers** agents.
15. **sightless** invisible.
16. **wait on** assist.
17. **pall** enshroud.
18. **dunnest** darkest.
19. **ignorant** unknowing.
20. **instant** present.
21. **beguile the time** deceive the people tonight.
22. **dispatch** management.

70 Give solely sovereign sway and masterdom.

MACBETH. We will speak further.

LADY MACBETH.   Only look up clear.[23]
To alter favor ever is to fear.[24]
Leave all the rest to me.   [*Exit.*]

Scene vi. Before Macbeth's castle.

[*Hautboys.*[1] *Torches. Enter* KING DUNCAN, MALCOLM,
DONALBAIN, BANQUO, LENNOX, MACDUFF, ROSS, ANGUS, *and*
ATTENDANTS.]

KING. This castle hath a pleasant seat;[2] the air
Nimbly and sweetly recommends itself
Unto our gentle[3] senses.

BANQUO.   This guest of summer,
The temple-haunting martlet,[4] does approve[5]
5   By his loved mansionry[6] that the heaven's breath
Smells wooingly here. No jutty,[7] frieze,
Buttress, nor coign of vantage,[8] but this bird
Hath made his pendent bed and procreant cradle.[9]
Where they most breed and haunt,[10] I have
   observed
The air is delicate.

[*Enter* LADY MACBETH.]

10   **KING.**   See, see, our honored hostess!
The love that follows us sometime is our trouble,
Which still we thank as love. Herein I teach you
How you shall bid God 'ield us for your pains
And thank us for your trouble.[11]

LADY MACBETH.   All our service

---

23. **look up clear** appear innocent.
24. **To alter . . . fear** to show a disturbed face will arouse suspicion.

---

1. *Hautboys* oboes announcing the arrival of royalty.
2. **seat** location.
3. **gentle** soothed.
4. **temple-haunting martlet** martin, a bird that usually nests in churches. In Shakespeare's time, martin was a slang term for a person who is easily deceived.
5. **approve** show.
6. **mansionry** nests.
7. **jutty** projection.
8. **coign of vantage** advantageous corner.
9. **procreant** (prō′ krē ənt) **cradle** nest where the young are hatched.
10. **haunt** visit.
11. **The love . . . trouble** Though my visit inconveniences you, you should ask God to reward me for coming, because it was my love for you that prompted my visit.

TAKE NOTES

15 In every point twice done, and then done double,
Were poor and single business[12] to contend
Against those honors deep and broad wherewith
Your Majesty loads our house: for those of old,
And the late dignities heaped up to them,
We rest your hermits.[13]

20 **KING.** Where's the Thane of Cawdor?
We coursed[14] him at the heels, and had a purpose
To be his purveyor:[15] but he rides well,
And his great love, sharp as his spur, hath holp[16] him
To his home before us. Fair and noble hostess,
We are your guest tonight.

25 **LADY MACBETH.** Your servants ever
Have theirs, themselves, and what is theirs, in compt,[17]
To make their audit at your Highness' pleasure,
Still[18] to return your own.

KING. Give me your hand.
Conduct me to mine host: we love him highly,
30 And shall continue our graces towards him.
By your leave, hostess. [*Exit.*]

Scene vii. Macbeth's castle.

[*Hautboys. Torches. Enter a* SEWER,[1] *and diverse* SERVANTS *with dishes and service over the stage. Then enter* MACBETH.]

MACBETH. If it were done[2] when 'tis done, then 'twere well
It were done quickly. If th' assassination
Could trammel up the consequence, and catch,
With his surcease, success;[3] that but this blow

---

12. **single business** feeble service.
13. **rest your hermits** remain your dependents bound to pray for you. Hermits were often paid to pray for another person's soul.
14. **coursed** chased.
15. **purveyor** advance supply officer.
16. **holp** helped.
17. **compt** trust.
18. **Still** always.

---

1. **sewer** chief butler.
2. **done** over and done with.
3. **If . . . success** if the assassination could be done successfully and without consequence.

5   Might be the be-all and the end-all—here,
    But here, upon this bank and shoal of time,
    We'd jump the life to come.[4] But in these cases
    We still have judgment here; that we but teach
    Bloody instructions, which, being taught, return
10 To plague th' inventor: this even-handed[5] justice
    Commends[6] th' ingredients of our poisoned chalice[7]
    To our own lips. He's here in double trust:
    First, as I am his kinsman and his subject,
    Strong both against the deed; then, as his host,
15 Who should against his murderer shut the door,
    Not bear the knife myself. Besides, this Duncan
    Hath borne his faculties[8] so meek, hath been
    So clear[9] in his great office, that his virtues
    Will plead like angels trumpet-tongued against
20 The deep damnation of his taking-off;
    And pity, like a naked newborn babe,
    Striding the blast, or heaven's cherubin[10] horsed
    Upon the sightless couriers[11] of the air,
    Shall blow the horrid deed in every eye,
25 That tears shall drown the wind. I have no spur
    To prick the sides of my intent, but only
    Vaulting ambition, which o'erleaps itself
    And falls on th' other—

[*Enter* LADY MACBETH.]

How now! What news?

LADY MACBETH. He has almost supped. Why have you
    left the chamber?

MACBETH. Hath he asked for me?

30 **LADY MACBETH.**   Know you not he has?

MACBETH. We will proceed no further in this
    business:
    He hath honored me of late, and I have bought[12]
    Golden opinions from all sorts of people,
    Which would be worn now in their newest gloss,
    Not cast aside so soon.

---

4. We'd . . . come I would risk life in the world to come.
5. even-handed impartial.
6. commends offers.
7. chalice cup.
8. faculties powers.
9. clear blameless.
10. cherubin angels.
11. sightless couriers unseen messengers (the wind).
12. bought acquired.

TAKE NOTES

35 **LADY MACBETH.**   Was the hope drunk
    Wherein you dressed yourself? Hath it slept since?
    And wakes it now, to look so green and pale
    At what it did so freely? From this time
    Such I account thy love. Art thou afeard
40 To be the same in thine own act and valor
    As thou art in desire? Wouldst thou have that
    Which thou esteem'st the ornament of life,[13]
    And live a coward in thine own esteem,
    Letting "I dare not" wait upon[14] "I would,"
    Like the poor cat i' th' adage?[15]

45 **MACBETH.**   Prithee, peace!
    I dare do all that may become a man;
    Who dares do more is none.

    LADY MACBETH.   What beast was 't then
    That made you break[16] this enterprise to me?
    When you durst do it, then you were a man;
50 And to be more than what you were, you would
    Be so much more the man. Nor time nor place
    Did then adhere,[17] and yet you would make both.
    They have made themselves, and that their[18]
       fitness now
    Does unmake you. I have given suck, and know
55 How tender 'tis to love the babe that milks me:
    I would, while it was smiling in my face,
    Have plucked my nipple from his boneless gums,
    And dashed the brains out, had I so sworn as you
    Have done to this.

    MACBETH.   If we should fail?

    LADY MACBETH.   We fail?
60 But[19] screw your courage to the sticking-place[20]
    And we'll not fail. When Duncan is asleep—
    Whereto the rather shall his day's hard journey
    Soundly invite him—his two chamberlains
    Will I with wine and wassail[21] so convince,[22]

---

13. **ornament of life** the crown.
14. **wait upon** follow.
15. **poor . . . adage** from an old proverb about a cat who wants to eat fish but is afraid of getting its paws wet.
16. **break** reveal.
17. **Did then adhere** was then suitable (for the assassination)
18. **that their** their very.
19. **But** only.
20. **sticking-place** the notch that holds the bowstring of a taut crossbow.
21. **wassail** carousing.
22. **convince** overpower.

65 That memory, the warder of the brain,
    Shall be a fume, and the receipt of reason
    A limbeck only:[23] when in swinish sleep
    Their drenchéd natures lies as in a death,
    What cannot you and I perform upon
70 Th' unguarded Duncan, what not put upon
    His spongy[24] officers, who shall bear the guilt
    Of our great quell?[25]

MACBETH.   Bring forth men-children only;
    For thy undaunted mettle[26] should compose
    Nothing but males. Will it not be received,
75 When we have marked with blood those sleepy two
    Of his own chamber, and used their very daggers,
    That they have done 't?

LADY MACBETH.   Who dares receive it other,[27]
    As we shall make our griefs and clamor roar
    Upon his death?

MACBETH.   I am settled, and bend up
80 Each corporal agent to this terrible feat.
    Away, and mock the time[28] with fairest show:
    False face must hide what the false heart doth
        know.   [*Exit.*]

---

23. That . . . only that memory, the guardian of the brain, will be confused by
the fumes of the drink, and the reason become like a still, distilling confused
thoughts.
24. spongy sodden.
25. quell murder.
26. mettle spirit.
27. other otherwise.
28. mock the time mislead the world.

TAKE NOTES

TAKE NOTES

Song

by John Donne

Sweetest love, I do not go,
    For weariness of thee,
Nor in hope the world can show
    A fitter love for me;
5   But since that I
Must die at last, 'tis best
To use[1] myself in jest,
    Thus by feigned[2] deaths to die.

Yesternight the sun went hence,
10   And yet is here today;
He hath no desire nor sense,
    Nor half so short a way;
        Then fear not me,
But believe that I shall make
15 Speedier journeys, since I take
    More wings and spurs than he.

O how feeble is man's power,
    That if good fortune fall,
Cannot add another hour,
20   Nor a lost hour recall!
        But come bad chance,
And we join to it our strength,
And we teach it art and length,
    Itself o'er us to advance.

25 When thou sigh'st, thou sigh'st not wind,
    But sigh'st my soul away;
When thou weep'st, unkindly kind,
    My life's blood doth decay.
        It cannot be
30 That thou lovest me as thou say'st,
If in thine my life thou waste,
    That art the best of me.

---

1. use condition.
2. feigned (fānd) *adj.* imagined.

Let not thy divining heart
        Forethink me any ill,
35 Destiny may take thy part,
        And may thy fears fulfill;
                But think that we
Are but turned aside to sleep.
They who one another keep
40   Alive, ne'r parted be.

TAKE NOTES

A Valediction:[1] Forbidding Mourning

by John Donne

As virtuous men pass mildly away,
    And whisper to their souls to go,
Whilst some of their sad friends do say
    The breath goes now, and some say, No;

5 So let us melt, and make no noise,
    No tear-floods, nor sigh-tempests move,
'Twere profanation of our joys
    To tell the laity our love.

Moving of th'earth brings harms and fears,
10   Men reckon what it did and meant;
But trepidation of the spheres,[2]
    Though greater far, is innocent.

Dull sublunary[3] lovers' love
    (Whose soul is sense) cannot admit
15 Absence, because it doth remove
    Those things which elemented it.[4]

But we by a love, so much refined,
    That our selves know not what it is,
Inter-assurèd of the mind,[5]
20   Care less, eyes, lips, and hands to miss.

Our two souls therefore, which are one,
    Though I must go, endure not yet
A breach, but an expansion,
    Like gold to airy thinness beat.

25 If they be two, they are two so
    As stiff twin compasses[6] are two;

---

1. **valediction** farewell speech.
2. **trepidation of the spheres** movements of the stars and planets that are inconsistent with a perfect circular orbit.
3. **sublunary** (sub′ loo nər′ ē) referring to the region below the moon, considered in early astronomy to be the domain of changeable and perishable things.
4. **Those things . . . elemented it** the basic materials or parts of their love.
5. **Inter-assurèd of the mind** mutually confident of each other's thoughts.
6. **twin compasses** the two legs of a drawing compass.

Thy soul the fixed foot, makes no show
    To move, but doth, if th'other do.

And though it in the center sit,
30   Yet when the other far doth roam,
It leans, and hearkens after it,
    And grows erect, as that comes home.

Such wilt thou be to me, who must
    Like th'other foot, obliquely[7] run;
35 Thy firmness makes my circle just,[8]
    And makes me end where I begun.

---

7. obliquely at an angle; not straight.
8. just true; perfect.

Holy Sonnet 10

by John Donne

BACKGROUND *Writers in Donne's day often depended on the support of patrons, wealthy supporters of the arts. The young Donne did not publish his poems (most were printed only after his death). Instead, they were circulated among a select literary audience that included patrons such as the Countess of Bedford. After Donne was dismissed from his position with Sir Thomas Egerton, he and his family depended in part on patrons for financial support. When he became a clergyman, Donne no longer needed to capture the interest of patrons. He continued, though, to write impassioned, witty verse such as the Holy Sonnets.*

> Death be not proud, though some have called thee
> Mighty and dreadful, for thou art not so;
> For those whom thou think'st thou dost overthrow,
> Die not, poor death, nor yet canst thou kill me.
> 5 From rest and sleep, which but thy pictures[1] be,
> Much pleasure; then from thee much more must
>   flow,
> And soonest our best men with thee do go,
> Rest of their bones, and soul's delivery.[2]
> Thou art slave to fate, chance, kings, and desperate
>   men,
> 10 And dost with poison, war, and sickness dwell,
> And poppy,[3] or charms can make us sleep as well
> And better than thy stroke; why swell'st[4] thou
>   then?
> One short sleep past, we wake eternally,
> And death shall be no more; Death, thou shalt die.

1. **pictures** images.
2. **And . . . delivery** Our best men go with you to rest their bones and find freedom for their souls.
3. **poppy** opium.
4. **swell'st** swell with pride.

Meditation 17

by John Donne

TAKE NOTES

Nunc lento sonitu dicunt, Morieris.
(Now, this bell tolling softly for another, says to
me, thou must die.)

Perchance he for whom this bell tolls may be so ill as that he knows not it tolls for him; and perchance I may think myself so much better than I am as that they who are about me and see my state may have caused it to toll for me, and I know not that. The church is catholic,[1] universal, so are all her actions; all that she does belongs to all. When she baptizes a child, that action concerns me; for that child is thereby connected to that head which is my head too, and ingrafted into that body[2] whereof I am a member. And when she buries a man, that action concerns me: all mankind is of one author and is one volume; when one man dies, one chapter is not torn out of the book, but translated into a better language; and every chapter must be so translated. God employs several translators; some pieces are translated by age, some by sickness, some by war, some by justice; but God's hand is in every translation, and his hand shall bind up all our scattered leaves again for that library where every book shall lie open to one another. As therefore the bell that rings to a sermon calls not upon the preacher only, but upon the congregation to come, so this bell calls us all; but how much more me, who am brought so near the door by this sickness. There was a contention as far as a suit[3] (in which both piety and dignity, religion and estimation,[4] were mingled) which of the religious orders should ring to prayers first in the morning; and it was determined that they should ring first that rose

---

1. **catholic** applying to humanity generally.
2. **head . . . body** In the Bible, St. Paul calls Jesus the head (spiritual leader) of all men (1 Corinthians 11:3) and a body in which the faithful are unified (1 Corinthians 12:12).
3. **suit** lawsuit.
4. **estimation** self-esteem.

TAKE NOTES

earliest. If we understand aright the dignity of this bell that tolls for our evening prayer, we would be glad to make it ours by rising early, in that application, that it might be ours as well as his whose indeed it is. The bell doth toll for him that thinks it doth; and though it intermit again, yet from that minute that that occasion wrought upon him, he is united to God. Who casts not up his eye to the sun when it rises? but who takes off his eye from a comet when that breaks out? Who bends not his ear to any bell which upon any occasion rings? but who can remove it from that bell which is passing a piece of himself out of this world? No man is an island, entire of itself; every man is a piece of the continent, a part of the main.[5] If a clod be washed away by the sea, Europe is the less, as well as if a promontory were, as well as if a manor of thy friend's or of thine own were. Any man's death diminishes me because I am involved in mankind, and therefore never send to know for whom the bell tolls; it tolls for thee. Neither can we call this a begging of misery or a borrowing of misery, as though we were not miserable enough of ourselves but must fetch in more from the next house, in taking upon us the misery of our neighbors. Truly it were an excusable covetousness if we did; for affliction is a treasure, and scarce any man hath enough of it. No man hath affliction enough that is not matured and ripened by it, and made fit for God by that affliction. If a man carry treasure in bullion, or in a wedge of gold, and have none coined into current money,[6] his treasure will not defray him as he travels. Tribulation is treasure in the nature of it, but it is not current money in the use of it, except we get nearer and nearer our home, heaven, by it. Another man may be sick too, and sick to death, and this affliction may lie in his bowels as gold in a mine and be of no use to him; but this bell that tells me of his affliction digs out and applies that gold to me, if by this consideration of another's danger, I take mine own into contemplation and so secure myself by making my recourse to my God, who is our only security.

---

5. **main** mainland.
6. **current money** currency; wealth in spendable form.

from the **Divine Comedy: Inferno**

by Dante Alighieri

BACKGROUND *In his* Divine Comedy, *Dante uses an organizing principle based on the number three, drawn from the Christian concept of the Holy Trinity. Documenting his imagined visit to Hell, Purgatory, and Heaven, he divides the epic into three parts—Inferno, Purgatorio, and Paradiso.*

In Paradise, Dante will be guided by his beloved Beatrice. For his trip through Hell to Purgatory, however, Dante's guide is the poet Virgil, to whom Dante pays homage by calling him "my Master." Virgil takes Dante through the nine circles of Hell, organized by gravity of the sin involved. In this final canto of Inferno, *the two reach the ninth circle, by the frozen waters of Cocytus1, where those guilty of the worst sin, treachery, are found. They include Judas Iscariot, who betrayed Jesus, and Brutus and Cassius, two Roman senators who plotted to assassinate the Roman leader Julius Caesar. They also include the angel-turned-devil Satan, here called Lucifer, the ultimate traitor who rebelled against God.*

Canto XXXIV

Ninth Circle: Cocytus	*Compound Fraud*
Round Four: Judecca	*The Treacherous to Their Masters*
The Center	*Satan*

"On march the banners of the King,"[2] Virgil begins as the Poets face the last depth. He is quoting a medieval hymn, and to it he adds the distortion and perversion of all that lies about him. "On march the banners of the King—of Hell." And there before them, in an infernal parody of Godhead, they see Satan in the distance, his great wings beating like a windmill. It is their beating that is the source of the icy wind of Cocytus, the exhalation of all evil.

---

1. **Cocytus** (kō sīt′ əs) Greek: "river of wailing."
2. **On ... King** This hymn was written in the sixth century by Venantius Fortunatus, Bishop of Poitiers. The original celebrates the Holy Cross and is part of the service for Good Friday, to be sung at the moment of uncovering the cross.

TAKE NOTES

TAKE NOTES

All about him in the ice are strewn the sinners of the last round, *Judecca,* named for Judas Iscariot.[3] These are the *Treacherous to Their Masters.* They lie completely sealed in the ice, twisted and distorted into every conceivable posture. It is impossible to speak to them, and the Poets move on to observe Satan.

He is fixed into the ice at the center to which flow all the rivers of guilt; and as he beats his great wings as if to escape, their icy wind only freezes him more surely into the polluted ice. In a grotesque parody of the Trinity, he has three faces, each a different color, and in each mouth he clamps a sinner whom he rips eternally with his teeth. *Judas Iscariot* is in the central mouth: *Brutus* and *Cassius*[4] in the mouths on either side.

Having seen all, the Poets now climb through the center, grappling hand over hand down the hairy flank of Satan himself—a last supremely symbolic action— and at last, when they have passed the center of all gravity, they emerge from Hell. A long climb from the earth's center to the Mount of Purgatory awaits them, and they push on without rest, ascending along the sides of the river Lethe, till they emerge once more to see the stars of Heaven, just before dawn on Easter Sunday.

> "On march the banners of the King of Hell,"
>   my Master said. "Toward us. Look straight
>   ahead:
>   can you make him out at the core of the frozen
>   shell?"
> Like a whirling windmill seen afar at twilight,
>
> 5   or when a mist has risen from the ground—
>   just such an engine rose upon my sight
>   stirring up such a wild and bitter wind
>   I cowered for shelter at my Master's back,
>   there being no other windbreak I could find.
> I stood now where the souls of the last class

---

3. **Judas Iscariot** (is ker′ ē ət) disciple who betrayed Jesus; see the Bible, Matthew 26:14, 48.
4. **Brutus and Cassius** They took part in a plot to assassinate Julius Caesar.

10   (with fear my verses tell it) were covered wholly;
          they shone below the ice like straws in glass.
      Some lie stretched out; others are fixed in place
          upright, some on their heads, some on their
              soles;
          another, like a bow, bends foot to face.
15   When we had gone so far across the ice
          that it pleased my Guide to show me the foul
              creature[5]
          which once had worn the grace of Paradise,
      he made me stop, and, stepping aside, he said:
          "Now see the face of Dis![6] This is the place
20   where you must arm your soul against all dread."
      Do not ask, Reader, how my blood ran cold
          and my voice choked up with fear. I cannot
              write it:
          this is a terror that cannot be told.
      I did not die, and yet I lost life's breath:
25   imagine for yourself what I became,
          deprived at once of both my life and death.
      The Emperor of the Universe of Pain
          jutted his upper chest above the ice;
          and I am closer in size to the great mountain
30   the Titans[7] make around the central pit,
          than they to his arms. Now, starting from this
              part,
          imagine the whole that corresponds to it!
      If he was once as beautiful as now
          he is hideous, and still turned on his Maker,
35   well may he be the source of every woe!
      With what a sense of awe I saw his head
          towering above me! for it had three faces:[8]
          one was in front, and it was fiery red;
      the other two, as weirdly wonderful,
40   merged with it from the middle of each
              shoulder
          to the point where all converged at the top of
              the skull;

---

5. the foul creature Lucifer.

6. Dis (dis) in Greek mythology, the god of the lower world or the lower world itself. Here, it stands for Lucifer.

7. Titans giant deities who were overthrown by Zeus and the Olympian gods of Greece.

8. three faces There are many interpretations of these three faces. The common theme in all of them is that the faces are a perversion of the qualities of the Trinity.

TAKE NOTES

TAKE NOTES

____
____
____
____
____
____
____
____
____
____
____
____
____
____
____
____
____
____
____
____
____
____
____
____

the right was something between white and bile;
    the left was about the color one observes
    on those who live along the banks of the Nile.
45 Under each head two wings rose terribly,
    their span proportioned to so gross a bird:
    I never saw such sails upon the sea.
They were not feathers—their texture and their
      form
    were like a bat's wings—and he beat them so
50   that three winds blew from him in one great
      storm:
it is these winds that freeze all Cocytus.
    He wept from his six eyes, and down three chins
    the tears ran mixed with bloody froth and pus.[9]
In every mouth he worked a broken sinner
55   between his rake-like teeth. Thus he kept three
    in eternal pain at his eternal dinner.
For the one in front the biting seemed to play
    no part at all compared to the ripping: at times
    the whole skin of his back was flayed away.
60 "That soul that suffers most," explained my Guide,
    "is Judas Iscariot, he who kicks his legs
    on the fiery chin and has his head inside.
Of the other two, who have their heads thrust
      forward,
    the one who dangles down from the black face
65   is Brutus: note how he writhes without a word.
And there, with the huge and sinewy arms, is the
      soul,
    of Cassius,—But the night is coming on[10]
    and we must go, for we have seen the whole."
Then, as he bade, I clasped his neck, and he,
70   watching for a moment when the wings
    were opened wide, reached over dexterously[11]
and seized the shaggy coat of the king demon;
    then grappling matted hair and frozen crusts
    from one tuft to another, clambered down.
75 When we had reached the joint where the great thigh
    merges into the swelling of the haunch,
    my Guide and Master, straining terribly,
turned his head to where his feet had been

---

9. bloody froth and pus the gore of the sinners he chews, which is mixed with his saliva.

10. the night is coming on It is now Saturday evening.

11. dexterously *adv.* skillfully.

and began to grip the hair as if he were climbing;[12]
80   so that I thought we moved toward Hell again.
"Hold fast!" my Guide said, and his breath came shrill

    with labor and exhaustion. "There is no way
    but by such stairs to rise above such evil."
At last he climbed out through an opening

85   in the central rock, and he seated me on the rim;
    then joined me with a nimble backward spring.
I looked up, thinking to see Lucifer

    as I had left him, and I saw instead
    his legs projecting high into the air.
90 Now let all those whose dull minds are still vexed

    by failure to understand what point it was
    I had passed through, judge if I was perplexed.
"Get up. Up on your feet," my Master said.

    "The sun already mounts to middle tierce,[13]
95   and a long road and hard climbing lie ahead."
It was no hall of state we had found there,

    but a natural animal pit hollowed from rock
    with a broken floor and a close and sunless air.
"Before I tear myself from the Abyss,"

100   I said when I had risen, "O my Master,
    explain to me my error in all this:
where is the ice? and Lucifer—how has he

    been turned from top to bottom: and how can the sun
    have gone from night to day so suddenly?"
105 And he to me: "You imagine you are still

    on the other side of the center where I grasped
    the shaggy flank of the Great Worm of Evil
which bores through the world—you were while I climbed down,

    but when I turned myself about, you passed
110   the point to which all gravities are drawn.
You are under the other hemisphere where you stand;

    the sky above us is the half opposed
    to that which canopies the great dry land.
Under the midpoint of that other sky

---

12. **as if he were climbing** They have passed the center of gravity and so must turn around and start climbing.

13. **middle tierce** According to the church's division of the day for prayer, tierce is the period from about six to nine A.M. Middle tierce, therefore, is seven-thirty. In going through the center point, Dante and Virgil have gone from night to day. They have moved ahead twelve hours.

TAKE NOTES

TAKE NOTES

115   the Man[14] who was born sinless and who lived
beyond all blemish, came to suffer and die.
You have your feet upon a little sphere
which forms the other face of the Judecca.
There it is evening when it is morning here.
120 And this gross Fiend and Image of all Evil
who made a stairway for us with his hide
is pinched and prisoned in the ice-pack still.
On this side he plunged down from heaven's height,
and the land that spread here once hid in the
sea
125 and fled North to our hemisphere for fright:[15]
And it may be that moved by that same fear,
the one peak[16] that still rises on this side
fled upward leaving this great cavern[17] here."
Down there, beginning at the further bound
130 of Beelzebub's[18] dim tomb, there is a space
not known by sight, but only by the sound
of a little stream[19] descending through the hollow
it has eroded from the massive stone
in its endlessly entwining lazy flow."
135 My Guide and I crossed over and began
to mount that little known and lightless road
to ascend into the shining world again.
He first, I second, without thought of rest
we climbed the dark until we reached the point
140 where a round opening brought in sight the
blest
and beauteous shining of the Heavenly cars.
And we walked out once more beneath the Stars.[20]

---

14. the Man Jesus, who suffered and died in Jerusalem, which was thought to be the middle of the Earth.

15. fled North . . . for fright Dante believed that the Northern Hemisphere was mostly land and the Southern Hemisphere, mostly water. Here, he explains the reason for this state of affairs.

16. the one peak the Mount of Purgatory.

17. this great cavern the natural animal pit of line 97. It is also "Beelzebub's dim tomb," line 130.

18. Beelzebub's (bē el′ zə bubz′) Beelzebub, which in Hebrew means "god of flies," was another name for Lucifer or Satan.

19. a little stream Lethe (lē′ thē); in classical mythology, the river of forgetfulness, from which souls drank before being born. In Dante's symbolism, it flows down from Purgatory, where it has washed away the memory of sin from the souls who are undergoing purification. That memory it delivers to Hell, which draws all sin to itself.

20. Stars As part of his total symbolism, Dante ends each of the three divisions of the *Divine Comedy* with this word. Every conclusion of the upward soul is toward the stars, symbols of hope and virtue. It is just before dawn of Easter Sunday that the Poets emerge—a further symbolism.

from Gulliver's Travels

by Jonathan Swift

TAKE NOTES

BACKGROUND *Swift's era was marked by religious and political strife. Reacting against the intolerance displayed in these conflicts, he ridiculed those whose pride overcame their reason. His novel* Gulliver's Travels *satirizes such intolerance by means of four imaginary voyages of Lemuel Gulliver, the narrator, a well-educated but unimaginative ship's surgeon. In "A Voyage to Lilliput," for example, Swift focuses on disputes between the established Church of England and Roman Catholicism, calling the followers of each Little-Endians and Big-Endians, respectively. He also satirizes the religious wars between Protestant England and Catholic France, disguising them as a conflict between Lilliput and Blefuscu. In "A Voyage to Brobdingnag," he suggests that the politicians leading England are guilty of "ignorance, idleness, and vice."*

from A Voyage to Lilliput

After being shipwrecked, Gulliver swims to shore and drifts off to sleep. When he awakens, he finds that he has been tied down by the Lilliputians (lil′ ə pyo͞o′ shənz), a race of people who are only six inches tall. Though he is held captive and his sword and pistols are taken from him, Gulliver gradually begins to win the Lilliputians' favor because of his mild disposition, and he is eventually granted his freedom. Through Gulliver's exposure to Lilliputian politics and court life, the reader becomes increasingly aware of the remarkable similarities between the English and Lilliputian affairs of state. The following excerpt begins during a discussion between the Lilliputian Principal Secretary of Private Affairs and Gulliver concerning the affairs of the Lilliputian empire.

TAKE NOTES

We are threatened with an invasion from the island of Blefuscu,[1] which is the other great empire of the universe, almost as large and powerful as this of his Majesty. For as to what we have heard you affirm, that there are other kingdoms and states in the world, inhabited by human creatures as large as yourself, our philosophers are in much doubt, and would rather conjecture that you dropped from the moon, or one of the stars; because it is certain, that an hundred mortals of your bulk would, in a short time, destroy all the fruits and cattle of his Majesty's dominions. Besides, our histories of six thousand moons make no mention of any other regions, than the two great empires of Lilliput and Blefuscu. Which two mighty powers have, as I was going to tell you, been engaged in a most obstinate war for six and thirty moons past. It began upon the following occasion. It is allowed on all hands, that the primitive way of breaking eggs before we eat them, was upon the larger end; but his present Majesty's grandfather, while he was a boy, going to eat an egg, and breaking it according to the ancient practice, happened to cut one of his fingers. Whereupon the Emperor, his father, published an edict, commanding all his subjects, upon great penalties, to break the smaller end of their eggs. The people so highly resented this law that our histories tell us there have been six rebellions raised on that account; wherein one emperor lost his life, and another his crown.[2] These civil commotions were constantly fomented by the monarchs of Blefuscu; and when they were quelled, the exiles always fled for refuge to that empire. It is computed that eleven thousand persons have, at several times, suffered death rather than submit to break their eggs at the smaller end. Many hundred large volumes have been published upon this controversy; but the books of the Big-Endians have been long forbidden, and the whole party rendered incapable by law of holding employments.[3] During the course of these troubles, the

---

1. **Blefuscu** represents France.
2. **It is allowed . . . crown** Here, Swift satirizes the dispute in England between the Catholics (Big-Endians) and Protestants (Little-Endians). King Henry VIII who "broke" with the Catholic church, King Charles I, who "lost his life," and King James, who lost his "crown," are each referred to in the passage.
3. **the whole party . . . employments** The Test Act (1673) prevented Catholics from holding office.

emperors of Blefuscu did frequently expostulate[4] by their ambassadors, accusing us of making a schism in religion, by offending against a fundamental doctrine of our great prophet Lustrog, in the fifty-fourth chapter of the *Brundecral* (which is their Alcoran).[5] This, however, is thought to be a mere strain upon the text, for the words are these: That all true believers shall break their eggs at the convenient end; and which is the convenient end, seems, in my humble opinion, to be left to every man's conscience, or at least in the power of the chief magistrate[6] to determine. Now the Big-Endian exiles have found so much credit in the Emperor of Blefuscu's court, and so much private assistance and encouragement from their party here at home, that a bloody war hath been carried on between the two empires for six and thirty moons with various success; during which time we have lost forty capital ships, and a much greater number of smaller vessels, together with thirty thousand of our best seamen and soldiers; and the damage received by the enemy is reckoned to be somewhat greater than ours. However, they have now equipped a numerous fleet, and are just preparing to make a descent upon us; and his Imperial Majesty, placing great confidence in your valor and strength, hath commanded me to lay this account of his affairs before you.

I desired the Secretary to present my humble duty to the Emperor, and to let him know, that I thought it would not become me, who was a foreigner, to interfere with parties; but I was ready, with the hazard of my life, to defend his person and state against all invaders.

The empire of Blefuscu is an island situated to the north-northeast side of Lilliput, from whence it is parted only by a channel of eight hundred yards wide. I had not yet seen it, and upon this notice of an intended invasion, I avoided appearing on that side of the coast, for fear of being discovered by some of the enemy's ships, who had received no intelligence of me, all intercourse between the two empires having been strictly forbidden during the war, upon pain of death, and an embargo laid by our Emperor upon all vessels whatsoever. I communicated to his Majesty a

---

4. **expostulate** (eks päs´ chə lāt´) *v.* reason earnestly with.
5. **Alcoran** Koran, the sacred book of Muslims.
6. **chief magistrate** ruler.

TAKE NOTES

project I had formed of seizing the enemy's whole fleet; which, as our scouts assured us, lay at anchor in the harbor ready to sail with the first fair wind. I consulted the most experienced seamen upon the depth of the channel, which they had often plumbed, who told me, that in the middle at high water it was seventy *glumgluffs* deep (which is about six feet of European measure), and the rest of it fifty *glumgluffs* at most. I walked to the northeast coast over against Blefuscu, where, lying down behind a hillock, I took out my small pocket perspective-glass, and viewed the enemy's fleet at anchor, consisting of about fifty men of war, and a great number of transports. I then came back to my house and gave order (for which I had a warrant) for a great quantity of the strongest cable and bars of iron. The cable was about as thick as packthread, and the bars of the length and size of a knitting-needle. I trebled the cable to make it stronger, and for the same reason I twisted three of the iron bars together, bending the extremities into a hook. Having thus fixed fifty hooks to as many cables, I went back to the northeast coast and, putting off my coat, shoes, and stockings, walked into the sea in my leathern jerkin, about half an hour before high water. I waded with what haste I could, and swam in the middle about thirty yards until I felt ground; I arrived at the fleet in less than half an hour. The enemy was so frightened when they saw me, that they leaped out of their ships, and swam to shore, where there could not be fewer than thirty thousand souls. I then took my tackling, and, fastening a hook to the hole at the prow of each, I tied all the cords together at the end. While I was thus employed, the enemy discharged several thousand arrows, many of which struck in my hands and face and, besides the excessive smart, gave me much disturbance in my work. My greatest apprehension was for my eyes, which I should have infallibly lost, if I had not suddenly thought of an expedient. I kept among other little necessaries a pair of spectacles in a private pocket, which, as I observed before, had escaped the Emperor's searchers. These I took out and fastened as strongly as I could upon my nose and thus armed went on boldly with my work in spite of the enemy's arrows, many of which struck against the glasses of my spectacles, but without any other effect further than a little to discompose them.

I had now fastened all the hooks and, taking the knot in my hand, began to pull, but not a ship would stir, for they were all too fast held by their anchors, so that the boldest part of my enterprise remained. I therefore let go the cord, and, leaving the hooks fixed to the ships, I resolutely cut with my knife the cables that fastened the anchors, receiving above two hundred shots in my face and hands; then I took up the knotted end of the cables to which my hooks were tied and, with great ease, drew fifty of the enemy's largest men-of-war after me.

The Blefuscudians, who had not the least imagination of what I intended, were at first confounded with astonishment. They had seen me cut the cables and thought my design was only to let the ships run adrift or fall foul on each other; but when they perceived the whole fleet, moving in order, and saw me pulling at the end, they set up such a scream of grief and despair that it is almost impossible to describe or conceive. When I had got out of danger, I stopped a while to pick out the arrows that stuck in my hands and face, and rubbed on some of the same ointment that was given me at my first arrival, as I have formerly mentioned. I then took off my spectacles, and, waiting about an hour until the tide was a little fallen, I waded through the middle with my cargo and arrived safe at the royal port of Lilliput.

The Emperor and his whole court stood on the shore expecting the issue of this great adventure. They saw the ships move forward in a large half-moon but could not discern me, who was up to my breast in water. When I advanced to the middle of the channel, they were yet more in pain, because I was under water to my neck. The Emperor concluded me to be drowned, and that the enemy's fleet was approaching in a hostile manner; but he was soon eased of his fears; for, the channel growing shallower every step I made, I came in a short time within hearing, and holding up the end of the cable by which the fleet was fastened, I cried in a loud voice, Long live the most puissant[7] Emperor of Lilliput! This great prince received me at my landing with all possible encomiums and created me a *Nardac* upon the spot, which is the highest title of honor among them.

---

7. **puissant** (pyo͞o′ i sənt) *adj.* powerful.

TAKE NOTES

His Majesty desired I would take some other opportunity of bringing all the rest of his enemy's ships into his ports. And so unmeasurable is the ambition of princes, that he seemed to think of nothing less than reducing the whole empire of Blefuscu into a province and governing it by a viceroy; of destroying the Big-Endian exiles and compelling that people to break the smaller end of their eggs, by which he would remain sole monarch of the whole world. But I endeavored to divert him from this design by many arguments drawn from the topics of policy as well as justice, and I plainly protested that I would never be an instrument of bringing a free and brave people into slavery. And when the matter was debated in council, the wisest part of the ministry were of my opinion.

This open bold declaration of mine was so opposite to the schemes and politics of his Imperial Majesty that he could never forgive me; he mentioned it in a very artful manner at council, where I was told that some of the wisest appeared, at least, by their silence, to be of my opinion; but others, who were my secret enemies, could not forbear some expressions, which by a sidewind reflected on me. And from this time began an intrigue between his Majesty and a junta of ministers maliciously bent against me, which broke out in less than two months and had like to have ended in my utter destruction. Of so little weight are the greatest services to princes when put into the balance with a refusal to gratify their passions.

from **A Voyage to Brobdingnag**

Gulliver's second voyage leads him to Brobdingnag (bräb′ diŋ nag′), an island located near Alaska that is inhabited by giants twelve times as tall as Gulliver. After being sold to the Queen of Brobdingnag, Gulliver describes the English social and political institutions to the King, who reacts to his description with contempt and disgust.

It is the custom that every Wednesday (which, as I have before observed, was their Sabbath) the King and Queen, with the royal issue of both sexes, dine together in the apartment of his Majesty, to whom I was now become a favorite; and at these times my little chair and table were placed at his left hand before one of the saltcellars. This prince took a pleasure in conversing with me, inquiring into the manners, religion, laws, government, and learning of Europe, wherein I gave him the best account I was able. His apprehension was so clear, and his judgment so exact, that he made very wise reflections and observations upon all I said. But I confess, that after I had been a little too copious in talking of my own beloved country, of our trade, and wars by sea and land, of our schisms in religion, and parties in the state, the prejudices of his education prevailed so far, that he could not forbear taking me up in his right hand, and stroking me gently with the other, after an hearty fit of laughing, asked me whether I were a Whig or a Tory.[8] Then turning to his first minister, who waited behind him with a white staff, near as tall as the mainmast of the *Royal Sovereign*,[9] he observed how contemptible a thing was human grandeur, which could be mimicked by such diminutive insects as I. And yet, said he, I dare engage, those creatures have their titles and distinctions of honor, they contrive little nests and burrows, that they call houses and cities; they make a figure in dress and equipage;[10] they love, they fight, they dispute, they cheat, they betray. And thus he continued on, while my color came and went several times, with indignation to hear our noble country, the mistress of arts and arms, the scourge of France, the arbitress of Europe, the seat of virtue, piety, honor and truth, the pride and envy of the world, so contemptuously treated. . . .

He laughed at my odd kind of arithmetic (as he was pleased to call it) in reckoning the numbers of our people by a computation drawn from the several sects among us in religion and politics. He said he knew no reason why those who entertain opinions prejudicial to the public should be obliged to change or should not be obliged to conceal them. And, as it was tyranny in any government to require the first, so it was weakness not to enforce the second; for, a man may be allowed to keep poisons in his closets, but not to vend them about as cordials.

---

8. **Whig . . . Tory** British political parties.
9. *Royal Sovereign* one of the largest ships in the British Navy.
10. **equipage** (ek′ wi pij′) horses and carriages.

from Gulliver's Travels **93**

TAKE NOTES

He observed, that among the diversions of our nobility and gentry[11] I had mentioned gaming.[12] He desired to know at what age this entertainment was usually taken up, and when it was laid down. How much of their time it employed; whether it ever went so high as to affect their fortunes. Whether mean vicious people by their dexterity in that art might not arrive at great riches, and sometimes keep our very nobles in dependence, as well as habituate them to vile[13] companions, wholly take them from the improvement of their minds, and force them, by the losses they received, to learn and practice that infamous dexterity upon others.

He was perfectly astonished with the historical account I gave him of our affairs during the last century, protesting it was only an heap of conspiracies, rebellions, murders, massacres, revolutions, banishments, the very worst effects that avarice, faction, hypocrisy, perfidiousness, cruelty, rage, madness, hatred, envy, lust, malice, and ambition could produce.

His Majesty in another audience was at the pains to recapitulate the sum of all I had spoken; compared the questions he made with the answers I had given; then taking me into his hands, and stroking me gently, delivered himself in these words, which I shall never forget, nor the manner he spoke them in. "My little friend Grildrig, you have made a most admirable panegyric upon your country. You have clearly proved that ignorance, idleness, and vice are the proper ingredients for qualifying a legislator. That laws are best explained, interpreted, and applied by those whose interest and abilities lie in perverting, confounding, and eluding them. I observe among you some lines of an institution, which in its original might have been tolerable, but these half erased, and the rest wholly blurred and blotted by corruptions. It doth not appear from all you have said how any one perfection is required toward the procurement of any one station among you, much less that men are ennobled on account of their virtue, that priests

---

11. gentry the class of landowning people ranking just below the nobility.
12. gaming gambling.
13. habituate (hə bich′ o͞o āt′) **them** to make them used to.

are advanced for their piety or learning, soldiers for their conduct or valor, judges for their integrity, senators for the love of their country, or counselors for their wisdom. As for yourself," continued the King, "who have spent the greatest part of your life in traveling, I am well disposed to hope you may hitherto have escaped many vices of your country. But, by what I have gathered from your own relation, and the answers I have with much pains wringed and extorted from you, I cannot but conclude the bulk of your natives to be the most pernicious race of little odious vermin that nature ever suffered to crawl upon the surface of the earth."

Nothing but an extreme love of truth could have hindered me from concealing this part of my story. It was in vain to discover my resentments, which were always turned into ridicule; and I was forced to rest with patience while my noble and most beloved country was so injuriously treated. I am heartily sorry as any of my readers can possibly be that such an occasion was given, but this prince happened to be so curious and inquisitive upon every particular that it could not consist either with gratitude or good manners to refuse giving him what satisfaction I was able. Yet thus much I may be allowed to say in my own vindication that I artfully eluded many of his questions and gave to every point a more favorable turn by many degrees than the strictness of truth would allow. For I have always borne that laudable partiality to my own country, which Dionysius Halicarnassensis[14] with so much justice recommends to an historian. I would hide the frailties and deformities of my political mother and place her virtues and beauties in the most advantageous light. This was my sincere endeavor in those many discourses I had with that mighty monarch, although it unfortunately failed of success.

But great allowances should be given to a king who lives wholly secluded from the rest of the world, and must therefore be altogether unacquainted with the manners and customs that most prevail in other nations: the want of which knowledge will ever

---

14. **Dionysius** (dī´ ə nish´ əs) **Halicarnassensis** (hal´ ə kär na sen´ sis) Greek writer who lived in Rome and attempted to persuade the Greeks to submit to their Roman conquerors.

TAKE NOTES

produce many prejudices, and a certain narrowness of thinking, from which we and the politer countries of Europe are wholly exempted. And it would be hard indeed, if so remote a prince's notions of virtue and vice were to be offered as a standard for all mankind.

To confirm what I have now said, and further to show the miserable effects of a confined education, I shall here insert a passage which will hardly obtain belief. In hopes to ingratiate myself farther into his Majesty's favor, I told him of an invention discovered between three and four hundred years ago, to make a certain powder, into an heap of which the smallest spark of fire falling, would kindle the whole in a moment, although it were as big as a mountain, and make it all fly up in the air together, with a noise and agitation greater than thunder. That a proper quantity of this powder rammed into an hollow tube of brass or iron, according to its bigness, would drive a ball of iron or lead with such violence and speed as nothing was able to sustain its force. That the largest balls, thus discharged, would not only destroy whole ranks of an army at once, but batter the strongest walls to the ground, sink down ships, with a thousand men in each, to the bottom of the sea; and when linked together by a chain, would cut through masts and rigging, divide hundreds of bodies in the middle, and lay all waste before them. That we often put this powder into large hollow balls of iron, and discharged them by an engine into some city we were besieging, which would rip up the pavement, tear the houses to pieces, burst and throw splinters on every side, dashing out the brains of all who came near. That I knew the ingredients very well, which were cheap, and common; I understood the manner of compounding them, and could direct his workmen how to make those tubes of a size proportionable to all other things in his Majesty's kingdom, and the largest need not be above two hundred foot long; twenty or thirty of which tubes, charged with the proper quantity of powder and balls, would batter down the walls of the strongest town in his dominions in a few hours, or destroy the whole metropolis, if ever it should pretend to dispute his absolute commands. This I humbly offered to his Majesty as a small tribute of acknowledgment in return of so many marks that I had received of his royal favor and protection.

The King was struck with horror at the description I had given of those terrible engines and the proposal I had made. He was amazed how so impotent and groveling an insect as I (these were his expressions) could entertain such inhuman ideas, and in so familiar a manner as to appear wholly unmoved at all the scenes of blood and desolation which I had painted as the common effects of those destructive machines; whereof he said some evil genius, enemy to mankind, must have been the first contriver. As for himself, he protested that although few things delighted him so much as new discoveries in art or in nature, yet he would rather lose half his kingdom than be privy to such a secret, which he commanded me, as I valued my life, never to mention any more.

TAKE NOTES

TAKE NOTES

The Aims of The Spectator

by Joseph Addison

It is with much satisfaction that I hear this great city inquiring day by day after these my papers, and receiving my morning lectures with a becoming seriousness and attention. My publisher tells me that there are already three thousand of them distributed every day. So that if I allow twenty readers to every paper, which I look upon as a modest computation, I may reckon about three-score thousand[1] disciples in London and Westminster, who I hope will take care to distinguish themselves from the thoughtless herd of their ignorant and unattentive brethren. Since I have raised to myself so great an audience, I shall spare no pains to make their instruction agreeable, and their diversion useful. For which reasons I shall endeavor to enliven morality with wit, and to temper wit with morality, that my readers may, if possible, both ways find their account in the speculation of the day. And to the end that their virtue and discretion may not be short, transient, intermitting[2] starts of thought, I have resolved to refresh their memories from day to day, till I have recovered them out of that desperate state of vice and folly into which the age is fallen. The mind that lies fallow[3] but a single day sprouts up in follies that are only to be killed by a constant and assiduous culture. It was said of Socrates[4] that he brought philosophy down from heaven, to inhabit among men; and I shall be ambitious to have it said of me that I have brought philosophy out of closets and libraries, schools and colleges, to dwell in clubs and assemblies, at tea tables and in coffeehouses.

I would therefore in a very particular manner recommend these my speculations to all well-regulated families that set apart an hour in every morning

---

1. **three-score thousand** sixty thousand.
2. **intermitting** pausing at times; not constant.
3. **fallow** unused; unproductive.
4. **Socrates** ancient Greek philosopher (470?–399 b.c.), immortalized as a character in Plato's dialogues, who cross-examined ancient Athenians about their lives and values.

for tea and bread and butter; and would earnestly advise them for their good to order this paper to be punctually served up, and to be looked upon as part of the tea equipage. . . .

In the next place, I would recommend this paper to the daily perusal of those gentlemen whom I cannot but consider as my good brothers and allies, I mean the fraternity of spectators, who live in the world without having anything to do in it; and either by the affluence of their fortunes or laziness of their dispositions have no other business with the rest of mankind but to look upon them. Under this class of men are comprehended all contemplative tradesmen, titular physicians, fellows of the Royal Society, Templars[5] that are not given to be contentious, and statesmen that are out of business; in short, everyone that considers the world as a theater, and desires to form a right judgment of those who are the actors on it.

There is another set of men that I must likewise lay a claim to, whom I have lately called the blanks of society, as being altogether unfurnished with ideas, till the business and conversation of the day has supplied them. I have often considered these poor souls with an eye of great commiseration, when I have heard them asking the first man they have met with, whether there was any news stirring? and by that means gathering together materials for thinking. These needy persons do not know what to talk of till about twelve o'clock in the morning; for by that time they are pretty good judges of the weather, know which way the wind sits, and whether the Dutch mail[6] be come in. As they lie at the mercy of the first man they meet, and are grave or impertinent all the day long, according to the notions which they have imbibed in the morning, I would earnestly entreat them not to stir out of their chambers till they have read this paper, and do promise them that I will daily instil into them such sound and wholesome sentiments as shall have a good effect on their conversation for the ensuing twelve hours.

---

5. **titular physicians, fellows of the Royal Society, Templars** physicians in title only; members of a group dedicated to scientific research; lawyers or law students with offices in the Inner or Middle Temple.
6. **Dutch mail** mail from Europe bearing news of the war.

TAKE NOTES

But there are none to whom this paper will be more useful than to the female world. I have often thought there has not been sufficient pains taken in finding out proper employments and diversions for the fair ones. Their amusements seem contrived for them, rather as they are women, than as they are reasonable creatures; and are more adapted to the sex than to the species. The toilet[7] is their great sense of business, and the right adjusting of their hair the principal employment of their lives. The sorting of a suit of ribbons is reckoned a very good morning's work; and if they make an excursion to a mercer's or a toyshop,[8] so great a fatigue makes them unfit for anything else all the day after. Their more serious occupations are sewing and embroidery, and their greatest drudgery the preparation of jellies and sweetmeats. This, I say, is the state of ordinary women; though I know there are multitudes of those of a more elevated life and conversation, that move in an exalted sphere of knowledge and virtue, that join all the beauties of the mind to the ornaments of dress, and inspire a kind of awe and respect, as well as love, into their male beholders. I hope to increase the number of these by publishing this daily paper, which I shall always endeavor to make an innocent if not an improving entertainment, and by that means at least divert the minds of my female readers from greater trifles. At the same time, as I would fain give some finishing touches to those which are already the most beautiful pieces in human nature, I shall endeavor to point all those imperfections that are the blemishes, as well as those virtues which are the embellishments, of the sex.

---

7. **toilet** act of dressing and grooming oneself.
8. **suit of ribbons . . . mercer's or a toyshop** A suit of ribbons was a set of matching ribbons; a mercer's store sold fabrics, ribbons, and so on; a toyshop sold small items of little value.

Introduction to **Frankenstein**

by Mary Wollstonecraft Shelley

BACKGROUND *In Greek mythology, Prometheus was one of the Titans—a race of giants who were said to have existed before humans and who engaged the gods in battle. Later myths say Prometheus created the first human beings. During the Romantic Era, Prometheus drew renewed attention. Percy Bysshe Shelley wrote a verse play about Prometheus entitled* Prometheus Unbound. *The complete title of Mary Shelley's novel about a doctor who attempts to create a man is* Frankenstein, or the Modern Prometheus.

The Publishers of the Standard Novels, in selecting *Frankenstein* for one of their series, expressed a wish that I should furnish them with some account of the origin of the story. I am the more willing to comply, because I shall thus give a general answer to the question, so very frequently asked me: "How I, then a young girl, came to think of, and to dilate upon, so very hideous an idea?" It is true that I am very averse to bringing myself forward in print; but as my account will only appear as an appendage to a former production, and as it will be confined to such topics as have connection with my authorship alone, I can scarcely accuse myself of a personal intrusion....

In the summer of 1816, we[1] visited Switzerland, and became the neighbors of Lord Byron. At first we spent our pleasant hours on the lake or wandering on its shores; and Lord Byron, who was writing the third canto of *Childe Harold,* was the only one among us who put his thoughts upon paper. These, as he brought them successively to us, clothed in all the light and harmony of poetry, seemed to stamp as divine the glories of heaven and earth, whose influences we partook with him.

---

1. we Mary Shelley, her husband Percy Bysshe Shelley, and their two children.

TAKE NOTES

But it proved a wet, ungenial summer, and incessant rain often confined us for days to the house. Some volumes of ghost stories, translated from the German into French,[2] fell into our hands. There was "The History of the Inconstant Lover,"[3] who, when he thought to clasp the bride to whom he had pledged his vows, found himself in the arms of the pale ghost of her whom he had deserted. There was the tale of the sinful founder of his race,[4] whose miserable doom it was to bestow the kiss of death on all the younger sons of his fated house, just when they reached the age of promise. His gigantic, shadowy form, clothed like the ghost in Hamlet, in complete armor but with the beaver[5] up, was seen at midnight, by the moon's fitful beams, to advance slowly along the gloomy avenue. The shape was lost beneath the shadow of the castle walls; but soon a gate swung back, a step was heard, the door of the chamber opened, and he advanced to the couch of the blooming youths, cradled in healthy sleep. Eternal sorrow sat upon his face as he bent down and kissed the foreheads of the boys, who from that hour withered like flowers snapped upon the stalk. I have not seen these stories since then, but their incidents are as fresh in my mind as if I had read them yesterday.

"We will each write a ghost story," said Lord Byron; and his proposition was acceded to. There were four of us.[6] The noble author began a tale, a fragment of which he printed at the end of his poem of Mazeppa. Shelley, more apt to embody ideas and sentiments in the radiance of brilliant imagery, and in the music of the most melodious verse that adorns our language, than to invent the machinery of a story, commenced one founded on the experiences of his early life. Poor Polidori had some terrible idea about a skull-headed lady, who was so punished for peeping through a keyhole—what to see I forget—something very shocking and wrong of course; but when she was reduced to a

---

2. **volumes . . . French** *Fantasmagoriana, or Collected Stories of Apparitions of Specters, Ghosts, Phantoms, Etc.,* published anonymously in 1812.
3. **"The History . . . Lover"** The true name of the story is "The Dead Fiancée."
4. **the tale . . . race** "Family Portraits."
5. **beaver** hinged piece of armor that covers the face.
6. **four of us** Byron, the two Shelleys, and John William Polidori, Byron's physician.

worse condition than the renowned Tom of Coventry,[7] he did not know what to do with her, and was obliged to despatch her to the tomb of the Capulets,[8] the only place for which she was fitted. The illustrious poets also, annoyed by the platitude of prose, speedily relinquished their uncongenial task.

I busied myself to *think of a story*—a story to rival those which had excited us to this task. One which would speak to the mysterious fears of our nature and awaken thrilling horror—one to make the reader dread to look round, to curdle the blood, and quicken the beatings of the heart. If I did not accomplish these things, my ghost story would be unworthy of its name. I thought and pondered—vainly. I felt that blank incapability of invention which is the greatest misery of authorship, when dull Nothing replies to our anxious invocations. *Have you thought of a story?* I was asked each morning, and each morning I was forced to reply with a mortifying negative....

Many and long were the conversations between Lord Byron and Shelley, to which I was a devout but nearly silent listener. During one of these, various philosophical doctrines were discussed, and among others the nature of the principle of life and whether there was any probability of its ever being discovered and communicated. They talked of the experiments of Dr. Darwin. (I speak not of what the Doctor really did or said that he did, but, as more to my purpose, of what was then spoken of as having been done by him), who preserved a piece of vermicelli in a glass case till by some extraordinary means it began to move with voluntary motion. Not thus, after all, would life be given. Perhaps a corpse would be reanimated: galvanism[9] had given token of such things. Perhaps the component parts of a creature might be manufactured, brought together, and endued with vital warmth.

Night waned upon this talk, and even the witching hour had gone by, before we retired to rest. When I placed my head on my pillow, I did not sleep, nor

---

7. **Tom of Coventry** "Peeping Tom" who, according to legend, was struck blind for looking at Lady Godiva as she rode naked through Coventry.
8. **tomb of the Capulets** the place where Romeo and Juliet died.
9. **galvanism** use of electric current to induce twitching in dead muscles.

TAKE NOTES

could I be said to think. My imagination, unbidden, possessed and guided me, gifting the successive images that arose in my mind with a vividness far beyond the usual bounds of reverie. I saw—with shut eyes but acute mental vision—I saw the pale student of unhallowed arts kneeling beside the thing he had put together. I saw the hideous phantasm of a man stretched out, and then, on the working of some powerful engine, show signs of life and stir with an uneasy, half vital motion. Frightful must it be, for supremely frightful would be the effect of any human endeavor to mock the stupendous mechanism of the Creator of the world. His success would terrify the artist; he would rush away from his odious handiwork, horror-stricken. He would hope that, left to itself, the slight spark of life which he had communicated would fade; that this thing, which had received such imperfect animation, would subside into dead matter; and he might sleep in the belief that the silence of the grave would quench forever the transient existence of the hideous corpse which he had looked upon as the cradle of life. He sleeps; but he is awakened; he opens his eyes; behold the horrid thing stands at his bedside, opening his curtains, and looking on him with yellow, watery, but speculative eyes.

I opened mine in terror. The idea so possessed my mind, that a thrill of fear ran through me, and I wished to exchange the ghastly image of my fancy for the realities around. I see them still: the very room, the dark parquet,[10] the closed shutters, with the moonlight struggling through, and the sense I had that the glassy lake and white high Alps were beyond. I could not so easily get rid of my hideous phantom: still it haunted me. I must try to think of something else. I recurred to my ghost story—my tiresome unlucky ghost story! O! if I could only contrive one which would frighten my reader as I myself had been frightened that night!

Swift as light and as cheering was the idea that broke in upon me. "I have found it! What terrified me will terrify others, and I need only describe the specter which had haunted my midnight pillow." On the morrow I announced that I had *thought of a story.*

---

10. **parquet** (pär kā´) flooring made of wooden pieces arranged in a pattern.

I began that day with the words, *It was on a dreary night of November,* making only a transcript of the grim terrors of my waking dream.

At first I thought but of a few pages—of a short tale—but Shelley urged me to develop the idea at greater length. I certainly did not owe the suggestion of one incident, nor scarcely of one train of feeling, to my husband, and yet but for his incitement, it would never have taken the form in which it was presented to the world. From this declaration I must except the preface. As far as I can recollect, it was entirely written by him.

And now, once again, I bid my hideous progeny go forth and prosper. I have an affection for it, for it was the offspring of happy days, when death and grief were but words, which found no true echo in my heart. Its several pages speak of many a walk, many a drive, and many a conversation, when I was not alone; and my companion was one who, in this world, I shall never see more. But this is for myself: my readers have nothing to do with these associations.

TAKE NOTES

TAKE NOTES

She Walks in Beauty

by George Gordon,
Lord Byron

BACKGROUND *Lord Byron became so identified with the rebellious heroes he created—brooding figures whose ironic attitude and hidden sorrow only added to their charm—that this kind of figure became known as a Byronic hero. Such heroes are a staple of Romantic literature. They survive in modern times as a Hollywood or rock-and-roll star.*

The Byronic attitude may be ironic, but Byron the poet was certainly capable of direct, sincere appreciation of beauty, as this poem demonstrates.

> She walks in beauty, like the night
>   Of cloudless climes and starry skies;
> And all that's best of dark and bright
>   Meet in her aspect and her eyes:
> 5 Thus mellowed to that tender light
>   Which heaven to gaudy day denies.
>
> One shade the more, one ray the less,
>   Had half impaired the nameless grace
> Which waves in every raven tress,
> 10   Or softly lightens o'er her face;
> Where thoughts serenely sweet express
>   How pure, how dear their dwelling place.
>
> And on that cheek, and o'er that brow,
>   So soft, so calm, yet eloquent,
> 15 The smiles that win, the tints that glow,
>   But tell of days in goodness spent,
> A mind at peace with all below,
>   A heart whose love is innocent!

from Childe Harold's Pilgrimage (Apostrophe to the Ocean)

by George Gordon,
Lord Byron

There is a pleasure in the pathless woods,
There is a rapture on the lonely shore,
There is society, where none intrudes,
By the deep sea, and music in its roar;
5   I love not man the less, but nature more,
From these our interviews, in which I steal
From all I may be, or have been before,
To mingle with the universe, and feel
What I can ne'er express, yet cannot all conceal.

10   Roll on, thou deep and dark blue ocean—roll!
Ten thousand fleets sweep over thee in vain;
Man marks the earth with ruin—his control
Stops with the shore; upon the watery plain
The wrecks are all thy deed, nor doth remain
15   A shadow of man's ravage, save[1] his own,
When, for a moment, like a drop of rain,
He sinks into thy depths with bubbling groan,
Without a grave, unknelled, uncoffined, and
unknown.

His steps are not upon thy paths—thy fields
20   Are not a spoil for him—thou dost arise
And shake him from thee; the vile strength he
wields
For earth's destruction thou dost all despise,
Spurning him from thy bosom to the skies,
And send'st him, shivering in thy playful spray
25   And howling, to his gods, where haply[2] lies
His petty hope in some near port or bay,
And dashest him again to earth—there let him lay.[3]

---

1. **save** except.
2. **haply** perhaps.
3. **lay** A note on Byron's proof suggests that he intentionally made this
grammatical error for the sake of the rhyme.

TAKE NOTES

____

____

____

____

____

____

____

____

____

____

____

____

____

____

____

____

____

____

____

The armaments which thunderstrike the walls
Of rock-built cities, bidding nations quake,
30   And monarchs tremble in their capitals,
The oak leviathans,[4] whose huge ribs make
Their clay creator[5] the vain title take
Of lord of thee, and arbiter of war—
These are thy toys, and, as the snowy flake,
35   They melt into thy yeast of waves, which mar
Alike the Armada's[6] pride or spoils of Trafalgar.[7]

Thy shores are empires, changed in all save thee—
Assyria, Greece, Rome, Carthage, what are they?
Thy waters washed them power while they were free,
40   And many a tyrant since; their shores obey
The stranger, slave, or savage: their decay
Has dried up realms to deserts—not so thou,
Unchangeable, save to thy wild waves' play.
Time writes no wrinkle on thine azure brow;
45   Such as creation's dawn beheld, thou rollest now.

Thou glorious mirror, where the Almighty's form
Glasses[8] itself in tempests: in all time,
Calm or convulsed—in breeze, or gale, or storm,
Icing the pole, or in the torrid clime
50   Dark-heaving—boundless, endless, and sublime;
The image of eternity, the throne
Of the Invisible; even from out thy slime
The monsters of the deep are made: each zone
Obeys thee; thou goest forth, dread, fathomless,[9] alone.

55   And I have loved thee, ocean! and my joy
Of youthful sports was on thy breast to be

---

4. **leviathans** (lə vī′ ə thənz) monstrous sea creatures, described in the Old Testament. Here the word means giant ships.
5. **clay creator** human beings.
6. **Armada's** refers to the Spanish Armada, defeated by the English in 1588.
7. **Trafalgar** battle in 1805 during which the French and Spanish fleets were defeated by the British fleet led by Lord Nelson.
8. **Glasses** mirrors.
9. **fathomless** (fath′ əm lis) *adj.* too deep to be measured or understood.

Borne, like thy bubbles, onward; from a boy
I wantoned with thy breakers—they to me
Were a delight: and if the freshening sea
Made them a terror—'twas a pleasing fear,
For I was as it were a child of thee,
And trusted to thy billows far and near,
And laid my hand upon thy mane—as I do here.

TAKE NOTES

from **Don Juan**

by George Gordon,
Lord Byron

BACKGROUND *Though it is unfinished, Don Juan (jōō´ ən) is regarded as Byron's finest work. A mock epic described by Shelley as "something wholly new and relative to the age," it satirizes the political and social problems of Byron's time.*

Traditionally Don Juan, the poem's hero, is a wicked character driven by his obsession with beautiful women. In Byron's work, Don Juan is an innocent young man whose physical beauty, charm, and spirit prove to be alluring to ladies. As a result, he finds himself in many difficult situations.

During periodic pauses in the story, the narrator drifts away from the subject. In these digressions the narrator comments on the issues of the time and on life in general. In this excerpt the narrator sets aside the adventures of his hero to reflect on old age and death.

But now at thirty years my hair is gray
(I wonder what it will be like at forty?
I thought of a peruke[1] the other day)—
My heart is not much greener; and in short, I
5 Have squandered my whole summer while
    'twas May,
And feel no more the spirit to retort; I
Have spent my life, both interest and principal,
And deem not, what I deemed, my soul
    invincible.

No more—no more—Oh! never more on me
10 The freshness of the heart can fall like dew,
Which out of all the lovely things we see
Extracts emotions beautiful and new,

---

1. peruke (pə rōōk´) wig.

Hived in our bosoms like the bag o' the bee:
Think'st thou the honey with those objects
   grew?
15 Alas! 'twas not in them, but in thy power
To double even the sweetness of a flower.

No more—no more—Oh! never more, my heart,
Canst thou be my sole world, my universe!
Once all in all, but now a thing apart,
20 Thou canst not be my blessing or my curse:
The illusion's gone forever, and thou art
Insensible,[2] I trust, but none the worse,
And in thy stead I've got a deal of judgment,
Though heaven knows how it ever found a
   lodgment.

25 My days of love are over; me no more
The charms of maid, wife, and still less of widow
Can make the fool of which they made before—
In short, I must not lead the life I did do;
The credulous hope of mutual minds is o'er,
30 The copious use of claret is forbid too,
So for a good old-gentlemanly vice,
I think I must take up with avarice.

Ambition was my idol, which was broken
Before the shrines of Sorrow and of Pleasure;
35 And the two last have left me many a token
O'er which reflection may be made at leisure:
Now, like Friar Bacon's brazen head, I've
   spoken,
"Time is, Time was, Time's past,"[3] a chymic[4]
   treasure
Is glittering youth, which I have spent betimes—
40 My heart in passion, and my head on rhymes.

What is the end of fame? 'tis but to fill
A certain portion of uncertain paper:
Some liken it to climbing up a hill,
Whose summit, like all hills, is lost in vapor;

---

2. **insensible** (in sen´ sə bəl) *adj.* unable to feel or sense anything; numb.
3. **Friar Bacon's . . . Time's past** In Robert Greene's comedy *Friar Bacon and Friar Bungay* (1594), these words are spoken by a bronze bust, made by Friar Bacon.
4. **chymic** (kim´ ik) alchemic: counterfeit.

TAKE NOTES

TAKE NOTES

45 For this men write, speak, preach, and heroes
   kill,
   And bards burn what they call their "midnight
   taper,"
   To have, when the original is dust,
   A name, a wretched picture, and worse bust.

   What are the hopes of man? Old Egypt's King
50 Cheops erected the first pyramid
   And largest, thinking it was just the thing
   To keep his memory whole, and mummy hid:
   But somebody or other rummaging
   Burglariously broke his coffin's lid:
55 Let not a monument give you or me hopes,
   Since not a pinch of dust remains of Cheops.

   But I, being fond of true philosophy,
   Say very often to myself, "Alas!
   All things that have been born were born to die,
60 And flesh (which Death mows down to hay) is
   grass;
   You've passed your youth not so unpleasantly,
   And if you had it o'er again—'twould pass—
   So thank your stars that matters are no worse,
   And read your Bible, sir, and mind your purse."

65 But for the present, gentle reader! and
   Still gentler purchaser! the bard—that's I—
   Must, with permission, shake you by the hand,
   And so your humble servant, and good-bye!
   We meet again, if we should understand
70 Each other; and if not, I shall not try
   Your patience further than by this short
   sample—
   'Twere well if others followed my example.

   "Go, little book, from this my solitude!
   I cast thee on the waters—go thy ways!
75 And if, as I believe, thy vein be good,
   The world will find thee after many days."[5]

---

5. Go . . . days lines from the last stanza of Robert Southey's (1774–1843)
Epilogue to *The Lay of the Laureate*.

When Southey's read, and Wordsworth
    understood,
I can't help putting in my claim to praise—
The four first rhymes are Southey's, every line:
For God's sake, reader! take them not for mine!

TAKE NOTES

On Making an Agreeable Marriage

by Jane Austen

To Fanny Knight [1]

Friday 18–Sunday 20 November 1814

Chawton Nov: 18.—Friday

I feel quite as doubtful as you could be my dearest Fanny as to *when* my Letter may be finished, for I can command very little quiet time at present, but yet I must begin, for I know you will be glad to hear as soon as possible, & I really am impatient myself to be writing something on so very interesting a subject, though I have no hope of writing anything to the purpose.—I shall do very little more I dare say than say over again, what you have said before.—I was certainly a good deal surprised *at first*—as I had no suspicion of any change in your feelings, and I have no scruple in saying that you cannot be in Love. My dear Fanny, I am ready to laugh at the idea— and yet it is no laughing matter to have had you so mistaken as to your own feelings—And with all my heart I wish I had cautioned you on that point when first you spoke to me;—but tho' I did not think you then so *much* in love as you thought yourself, I did consider you as being attached in a degree—quite sufficiently for happiness, as I had no doubt it would increase with opportunity.—And from the time of our being in London together, I thought you really very much in love.—But you certainly are not at all— there is no concealing it.—What strange creatures we are!—It seems as if your being secure of him (as you say yourself) had made you Indifferent.—There was a little disgust I suspect, at the Races—& I do

---

1. **Fanny Knight** Fanny Austen Knight was the daughter of Austen's brother Edward.

not wonder at it. His expressions then would not do for one who had rather more Acuteness, Penetration & Taste, than Love, which was your case. And yet, after all, I *am* surprised that the change in your feelings should be so great.—He is, just what he ever was, only more evidently & uniformly devoted to *you*. This is all the difference.—How shall we account for it?—My dearest Fanny, I am writing what will not be of the smallest use to you. I am feeling differently every moment, & shall not be able to suggest a single thing that can assist your Mind.—I could lament in one sentence & laugh in the next, but as to Opinion or Counsel I am sure none will [be] extracted worth having from this Letter.—I read yours through the very even[2] I received it—getting away by myself—I could not bear to leave off, when I had once begun.—I was full of curiosity & concern. Luckily Your Aunt C. dined at the other house, therefore I had not to maneuver away from *her;*—& as to anybody else, I do not care.—Poor dear Mr J. P![3]—Oh! dear Fanny, Your mistake has been one that thousands of women fall into. He was the *first* young Man who attached himself to you. That was the charm, & most powerful it is.—Among the multitudes however that make the same mistake with Yourself, there can be few indeed who have so little reason to regret it;—*his* Character & *his* attachment leave you nothing to be ashamed of.—Upon the whole, what is to be done? You certainly *have* encouraged him to such a point as to make him feel almost secure of you—you have no inclination for any other person—His situation in life, family, friends, & above all his Character—his uncommonly amiable mind, strict principles, just notions, good habits—*all* that *you* know so well how to value, *All* that really is of the first importance—everything of this nature pleads his cause most strongly.—You have no doubt of his having superior Abilities—he has proved it at the University—he is I dare say such a Scholar as your agreeable, idle Brothers would ill bear a comparison with.—Oh! my dear Fanny, the more I write about him, the warmer my feelings become,

---

2. **even** evening.
3. **Mr J. P.** Fanny's suitor.

TAKE NOTES

the more strongly I feel the sterling worth of such a young Man & the desirableness of your growing in love with him again. I recommend this most thoroughly.— There *are* such beings in the World perhaps, one in a Thousand, as the Creature You & I should think perfection, where Grace & Spirit are united to Worth, where the Manners are equal to the Heart & Understanding, but such a person may not come in your way, or if he does, he may not be the eldest son of a Man of Fortune, the Brother of your particular friend, & belonging to your own County.—Think of all this Fanny. Mr J. P.– has advantages which do not often meet in one person. His only fault indeed seems Modesty. If he were less modest, he would be more agreeable, speak louder & look Impudenter;—and is not it a fine Character, of which Modesty is the only defect?—I have no doubt that he will get more lively & more like yourselves as he is more with you;—he will catch your ways if he belongs to you. And as to there being any objection from his *Goodness*, from the danger of his becoming even Evangelical,[4] I cannot admit *that*. I am by no means convinced that we ought not all to be Evangelicals, & am at least persuaded that they who are so from Reason & Feeling, must be happiest & safest.—Do not be frightened from the connection by your Brothers having most wit. Wisdom is better than Wit, & in the long run will certainly have the laugh on her side; & don't be frightened by the idea of his acting more strictly up to the precepts of the New Testament than others.— And now, my dear Fanny, having written so much on one side of the question, I shall turn round & entreat you not to commit yourself farther, & not to think of accepting him unless you really do like him. Anything is to be preferred or endured rather than marrying without Affection; and if his deficiencies of Manner &c &c[5] strike you more than all his good qualities, if you continue to think strongly of them, give him up at once.—Things are now in such a state, that you must

---

4. **Evangelical** of or relating to a group of earnest Church of England members active in social reform movements at the time of the letter.
5. **&c &c** et cetera (the & symbol, called an ampersand, stands for et, Latin for "and").

resolve upon one or the other, either to allow him to go on as he has done, or whenever you are together behave with a coldness which may convince him that he has been deceiving himself.—I have no doubt of his suffering a good deal for a time, a great deal, when he feels that he must give you up;—but it is no creed of mine, as you must be well aware, that such sort of Disappointments kill anybody.—Your sending the Music was an admirable device,[6] it made everything easy, & I do not know how I could have accounted for the parcel otherwise; for tho' your dear Papa most conscientiously hunted about till he found me alone in the Din^g-parlor,[7] Your Aunt C. had seen that he had a parcel to deliver.—As it was however, I do not think anything was suspected.—We have heard nothing fresh from Anna. I trust she is very comfortable in her new home. Her Letters have been very sensible & satisfactory, with no *parade* of happiness, which I liked them the better for.—I have often known young married Women write in a way I did not like, in that respect.

You will be glad to hear that the first Edit: of M.P.[8] is all sold.—Your Uncle Henry is rather wanting me to come to Town, to settle about a 2^d Edit:—but as I could not very conveniently leave home now, I have written him my Will & pleasure, & unless he still urges it, shall not go.—I am very greedy & want to make the most of it;—but as you are much above caring about money, I shall not plague you with any particulars.—The pleasures of Vanity are more within your comprehension, & you will enter into mine, at receiving the *praise* which every now & then comes to me, through some channel or other.—

---

6. **device** trick; ruse; ploy.
7. **Din^g-parlor** dining room.
8. **M.P.** Austen's novel *Mansfield Park*.

TAKE NOTES

from A Vindication of the Rights of Woman

by Mary Wollstonecraft

BACKGROUND *British women in the eighteenth and early nineteenth centuries had few economic or legal rights. In most cases, a woman's property was legally her father's until she married, after which the property became her husband's. Women's education focused mainly on "ladylike" accomplishments such as sewing and music. Women who showed an interest in things beyond marriage and the home were generally regarded as unfeminine. Mary Wollstonecraft focuses on the deforming effects that inadequate education had on women of her time and indicates the larger social forces holding women back.*

After considering the historic page,[1] and viewing the living world with anxious solicitude the most melancholy emotions of sorrowful indignation have depressed my spirits, and I have sighed when obliged to confess that either Nature has made a great difference between man and man,[2] or that the civilization which has hitherto taken place in the world has been very partial. I have turned over various books written on the subject of education, and patiently observed the conduct of parents and the management of schools; but what has been the result?—a profound conviction that the neglected education of my fellow creatures is the grand source of the misery I deplore, and that women, in particular, are rendered weak and wretched by a variety of concurring causes, originating from one hasty conclusion. The conduct and manners of women, in fact, evidently prove that their minds are not in a healthy state; for, like the flowers which are planted in too rich a soil, strength and usefulness are sacrificed to beauty; and the flaunting leaves, after having pleased a fastidious eye, fade, disregarded on

---

1. **the historic page** the record of history.
2. **man and man** used here in the generic sense to mean "human being and human being."

the stalk, long before the season when they ought to
have arrived at maturity. One cause of this barren
blooming I attribute to a false system of education,
gathered from the books written on this subject
by men who, considering females rather as women
than human creatures, have been more anxious to
make them alluring ... than affectionate wives and
rational mothers; and the understanding of the sex
has been so bubbled by this specious homage, that
the civilized women of the present century, with a few
exceptions, are only anxious to inspire love, when
they ought to cherish a nobler ambition, and by their
abilities and virtues exact respect ... .

The education of women has of late been more
attended to than formerly; yet they are still reckoned
a frivolous sex, and ridiculed or pitied by the writers
who endeavor by satire or instruction to improve
them. It is acknowledged that they spend many of the
first years of their lives in acquiring a smattering of
accomplishments; meanwhile strength of body and
mind are sacrificed to libertine[3] notions of beauty, to
the desire of establishing themselves—the only way
women can rise in the world—by marriage. And this
desire making mere animals of them, when they marry
they act as such children may be expected to act—they
dress, they paint, and nickname God's creatures. ...
Can they be expected to govern a family with judgment,
or take care of the poor babes whom they bring into
the world?

If, then, it can be fairly deduced from the present
conduct of the sex, from the prevalent fondness for
pleasure which takes place of ambition and those
nobler passions that open and enlarge the soul, that
the instruction which women have hitherto received
has only tended, with the constitution of civil society,
to render them insignificant objects of desire—mere
propagators of fools!—if it can be proved that in
aiming to accomplish them, without cultivating their
understandings, they are taken out of their sphere
of duties, and made ridiculous and useless when
the short-lived bloom of beauty is over, I presume
that *rational* men will excuse me for endeavoring

---

3. libertine immoral.

TAKE NOTES

to persuade them to become more masculine and respectable.

Indeed the word masculine is only a bugbear;[4] there is little reason to fear that women will acquire too much courage or fortitude, for their apparent inferiority with respect to bodily strength must render them in some degree dependent on men in the various relations of life; but why should it be increased by prejudices that give a sex to virtue, and confound simple truths with sensual reveries?

Women are, in fact, so much degraded by mistaken notions of female excellence, that I do not mean to add a paradox when I assert that this artificial weakness produces a propensity to tyrannize, and gives birth to cunning, the natural opponent of strength, which leads them to play off those contemptible infantine[5] airs that undermine esteem even whilst they excite desire. Let me become more chaste and modest, and if women do not grow wiser in the same ratio it will be clear that they have weaker understandings. It seems scarcely necessary to say that I now speak of the sex in general. Many individuals have more sense than their male relatives; and, as nothing preponderates where there is a constant struggle for an equilibrium without it has[6] naturally more gravity, some women govern their husbands without degrading themselves, because intellect will always govern.

---

4. **bugbear** frightening imaginary creature, especially one that frightens children.
5. **infantine** infantile; childish.
6. **without it has** without having.

My Last Duchess

by Robert Browning

BACKGROUND *This poem, set in the sixteenth century in a castle in northern Italy, is based on events from the life of the duke of Ferrara, a nobleman whose first wife died after just three years of marriage. Following his wife's death, the duke began making arrangements to remarry. In Browning's poem, the duke is showing a painting of his first wife to an agent who represents the father of the woman he hopes to marry.*

That's my last Duchess painted on the wall,
Looking as if she were alive. I call
That piece a wonder, now: Frà Pandolf's[1] hands
Worked busily a day, and there she stands.
5 Will't please you sit and look at her? I said
"Frà Pandolf" by design, for never read
Strangers like you that pictured countenance
The depth and passion of its earnest glance,
But to myself they turned (since none puts by
10 The curtain I have drawn for you, but I)
And seemed as they would ask me, if they durst,[2]
How such a glance came there; so, not the first
Are you to turn and ask thus. Sir, 'twas not
Her husband's presence only, called that spot
15 Of joy into the Duchess' cheek: perhaps
Frà Pandolf chanced to say "Her mantle laps
Over my lady's wrist too much," or "Paint
Must never hope to reproduce the faint
Half-flush that dies along her throat"; such stuff
20 Was courtesy, she thought, and cause enough
For calling up that spot of joy. She had
A heart—how shall I say?—too soon made glad,
Too easily impressed; she liked whate'er
She looked on, and her looks went everywhere.
25 Sir, 'twas all one! My favor at her breast,
The dropping of the daylight in the West,

---

1. Frà Pandolf's work of Brother Pandolf, an imaginary painter.
2. durst dared.

TAKE NOTES

The bough of cherries some officious fool
Broke in the orchard for her, the white mule
She rode with round the terrace—all and each
30 Would draw from her alike the approving speech,
  Or blush, at least. She thanked men—good! but thanked
Somehow—I know not how—as if she ranked
My gift of a nine-hundred-year-old name
With anybody's gift. Who'd stoop to blame
35 This sort of trifling? Even had you skill
In speech—(which I have not)—to make your will
Quite clear to such an one, and say, "Just this
Or that in you disgusts me; here you miss,
Or there exceed the mark"—and if she let
40 Herself be lessoned so, nor plainly set
Her wits to yours, forsooth,[3] and made excuse,
—E'en then would be some stooping; and I choose
Never to stoop. Oh sir, she smiled, no doubt,
Whene'er I passed her; but who passed without
45 Much the same smile? This grew; I gave commands;
Then all smiles stopped together. There she stands
As if alive. Will 't please you rise? We'll meet
The company below, then. I repeat,
The Count your master's known munificence
50 Is ample warrant that no one just pretense
Of mine for dowry will be disallowed;
Though his fair daughter's self, as I avowed
At starting, is my object. Nay, we'll go
Together down, sir! Notice Neptune,[4] though,
55 Taming a sea horse, thought a rarity,
Which Claus of Innsbruck[5] cast in bronze for me!

---

3. forsooth in truth.
4. Neptune in Roman mythology, the god of the sea.
5. Claus of Innsbruck imaginary Austrian sculptor.

Life in a Love

by Robert Browning

Escape me?
    Never—
    Beloved!
While I am I, and you are you,
5   So long as the world contains us both,
     Me the loving and you the loth,
While the one eludes, must the other pursue.
My life is a fault at last, I fear:
It seems too much like a fate, indeed!
10 Though I do my best I shall scarce succeed.
But what if I fail of my purpose here?
It is but to keep the nerves at strain,
To dry one's eyes and laugh at a fall,
And, baffled, get up and begin again,—
15 So the chase takes up one's life, that's all.
While, look but once from your farthest bound
At me so deep in the dust and dark,
No sooner the old hope goes to ground
Than a new one, straight to the self-same mark,
20 I shape me—
Ever
Removed!

TAKE NOTES

____

____

____

____

____

____

____

____

____

____

____

____

____

____

____

____

____

____

____

Porphyria's Lover

by Robert Browning

The rain set early in tonight,
    The sullen wind was soon awake,
It tore the elm-tops down for spite,
    And did its worst to vex the lake:
5   I listened with heart fit to break.
When glided in Porphyria; straight
    She shut the cold out and the storm,
And kneeled and made the cheerless grate
    Blaze up, and all the cottage warm;
10   Which done, she rose, and from her form
Withdrew the dripping cloak and shawl,
    And laid her soiled gloves by, untied
Her hat and let the damp hair fall,
    And, last, she sat down by my side
15   And called me. When no voice replied,
She put my arm about her waist,
    And made her smooth white shoulder bare,
And all her yellow hair displaced,
    And, stooping, made my cheek lie there,
20   And spread, o'er all, her yellow hair,
Murmuring how she loved me—she
    Too weak, for all her heart's endeavor,
To set its struggling passion free
    From pride, and vainer ties dissever,
25   And give herself to me for ever.
But passion sometimes would prevail,
    Nor could tonight's gay feast restrain
A sudden thought of one so pale
    For love of her, and all in vain:
30   So, she was come through wind and rain.
Be sure I looked up at her eyes
    Happy and proud; at last I knew
Porphyria worshipped me; surprise
    Made my heart swell, and still it grew
35   While I debated what to do.
That moment she was mine, mine, fair,
    Perfectly pure and good: I found

A thing to do, and all her hair
    In one long yellow string I wound
40   Three times her little throat around,
And strangled her. No pain felt she;
    I am quite sure she felt no pain.
As a shut bud that holds a bee,
    I warily oped her lids: again
45   Laughed the blue eyes without a stain.
And I untightened next the tress
    About her neck; her cheek once more
Blushed bright beneath my burning kiss:
    I propped her head up as before,
50   Only, this time my shoulder bore
Her head, which droops upon it still:
    The smiling rosy little head,
So glad it has its utmost will,
    That all it scorned at once is fled,
55   And I, its love, am gained instead!
Porphyria's love: she guessed not how
    Her darling one wish would be heard.
And thus we sit together now,
    And all night long we have not stirred,
60   And yet God has not said a word!

TAKE NOTES

Sonnet 43

By Elizabeth Barrett Browning

How do I love thee? Let me count the ways.
I love thee to the depth and breadth and height
My soul can reach, when feeling out of sight
For the ends of Being and ideal Grace.
5 I love thee to the level of every day's
Most quiet need, by sun and candlelight.
I love thee freely, as men strive for Right;
I love thee purely, as they turn from Praise.
I love thee with the passion put to use
10 In my old griefs, and with my childhood's faith.
I love thee with a love I seemed to lose
With my lost saints—I love thee with the breath,
Smiles, tears, of all my life!—and, if God choose,
I shall but love thee better after death.

from **Jane Eyre**

by Charlotte Brontë

CHAPTER 6

The next day commenced as before, getting up and dressing by rushlight; but this morning we were obliged to dispense with the ceremony of washing: the water in the pitchers was frozen. A change had taken place in the weather the preceding evening, and a keen northeast wind, whistling through the crevices of our bedroom windows all night long, had made us shiver in our beds, and turned the contents of the ewers to ice.

Before the long hour and a half of prayers and Bible reading was over, I felt ready to perish with cold. Breakfast time came at last, and this morning the porridge was not burnt; the quality was eatable, the quantity small; how small my portion seemed! I wished it had been doubled.

In the course of the day I was enrolled a member of the fourth class, and regular tasks and occupations were assigned to me: hitherto, I had only been a spectator of the proceedings at Lowood, I was now to become an actor therein. At first, being little accustomed to learn by heart, the lessons appeared to me both long and difficult: the frequent change from task to task, too, bewildered me; and I was glad, when, about three o'clock in the afternoon, Miss Smith put into my hands a border of muslin two yards long, together with needle, thimble, etc., and sent me to sit in a quiet corner of the school room, with directions to hem the same. At that hour most of the others were sewing likewise; but one class still stood round Miss Scatcherd's chair reading, and as all was quiet, the subject of their lessons could be heard, together with the manner in which each girl acquitted herself, and the animadversions or commendations of Miss Scatcherd on the performance. It was English history; among the readers, I observed my acquaintance of the

TAKE NOTES

verandah; at the commencement of the lesson, her place had been at the top of the class, but for some error of pronunciation or some inattention to stops, she was suddenly sent to the very bottom. Even in that obscure position, Miss Scatcherd continued to make her an object of constant notice: she was continually addressing to her such phrases as the following:—

"Burns" (such it seems was her name: the girls here, were all called by their surnames, as boys are elsewhere), "Burns, you are standing on the side of your shoe, turn your toes out immediately." "Burns, you poke your chin most unpleasantly, draw it in." "Burns, I insist on your holding your head up: I will not have you before me in that attitude," etc. etc.

A chapter having been read through twice, the books were closed and the girls examined. The lesson had comprised part of the reign of Charles I, and there were sundry questions about tonnage and poundage, and ship-money, which most of them appeared unable to answer; still, every little difficulty was solved instantly when it reached Burns: her memory seemed to have retained the substance of the whole lesson, and she was ready with answers on every point. I kept expecting that Miss Scatcherd would praise her attention; but, instead of that, she suddenly cried out:—

"You dirty, disagreeable girl! you have never cleaned your nails this morning!"

Burns made no answer: I wondered at her silence.

"Why," thought I, "does she not explain that she could neither clean her nails nor wash her face, as the water was frozen?"

My attention was now called off by Miss Smith, desiring me to hold a skein of thread: while she was winding it, she talked to me from time to time, asking whether I had ever been at school before, whether I could mark, stitch, knit, etc.; till she dismissed me, I could not pursue my observations on Miss Scatcherd's movements. When I returned to my seat, that lady was just delivering an order, of which I did not catch the import; but Burns immediately left the class, and going into the small inner room where the books were kept, returned in half a minute, carrying in her hand a bundle of twigs tied together at one end. This ominous tool she presented to Miss Scatcherd with a respectful courtesy; then she quietly, and without being told, unloosed her pinafore, and the teacher instantly and sharply inflicted on her neck a dozen strokes with the bunch of twigs. Not a tear rose to Burns's eye; and, while I paused from my sewing, because my fingers quivered at this spectacle with a sentiment of unavailing and impotent anger, not a feature of her pensive face altered its ordinary expression.

"Hardened girl!" exclaimed Miss Scatcherd, "nothing can correct you of your slatternly habits: carry the rod away."

Burns obeyed: I looked at her narrowly as she emerged from the book closet; she was just putting back her handkerchief into her pocket, and the trace of a tear glistened on her thin cheek.

The play hour in the evening I thought the pleasantest fraction of the day at Lowood: the bit of bread, the draught of coffee swallowed at five o'clock had revived vitality, if it had not satisfied hunger; the long restraint of the day was slackened; the school room felt warmer than in the morning: its fires being allowed to burn a little more brightly to supply, in some measure, the place of candles, not yet introduced; the ruddy gloaming,[1] the licensed uproar, the confusion of many voices gave one a welcome sense of liberty.

On the evening of the day on which I had seen Miss Scatcherd flog her pupil, Burns, I wandered as usual among the forms and tables and laughing groups without a companion, yet not feeling lonely: when I passed the windows, I now and then lifted a blind and looked out; it snowed fast, a drift was already forming against the lower panes; putting my ear close to the window, I could distinguish from the gleeful tumult within, the disconsolate moan of the wind outside.

Probably, if I had lately left a good home and kind parents, this would have been the hour when I should most keenly have regretted the separation: that wind would then have saddened my heart; this obscure chaos would have disturbed my peace: as it was I

---

1. **ruddy gloaming** glowing twilight; the sunset.

TAKE NOTES

derived from both a strange excitement, and reckless and feverish, I wished the wind to howl more wildly, the gloom to deepen to darkness, and the confusion to rise to clamor.

Jumping over forms, and creeping under tables, I made my way to one of the fire-places: there, kneeling by the high wire fender, I found Burns, absorbed, silent, abstracted from all round her by the companionship of a book, which she read by the dim glare of the embers.

"Is it still 'Rasselas'?"[2] I asked, coming behind her.

"Yes," she said, "and I have just finished it."

And in five minutes more she shut it up. I was glad of this.

"Now," thought I, "I can perhaps get her to talk." I sat down by her on the floor.

"What is your name besides Burns?"

"Helen."

"Do you come a long way from here?"

"I come from a place further north; quite on the borders of Scotland."

"Will you ever go back?"

"I hope so; but nobody can be sure of the future."

"You must wish to leave Lowood?"

"No: why should I? I was sent to Lowood to get an education; and it would be of no use going away until I have attained that object."

"But that teacher, Miss Scatcherd, is so cruel to you?"

"Cruel? Not at all! She is severe: she dislikes my faults."

"And if I were in your place I should dislike her: I should resist her; if she struck me with that rod, I should get it from her hand; I should break it under her nose."

"Probably you would do nothing of the sort: but if you did, Mr. Brocklehurst would expel you from the school; that would be a great grief to your relations. It is far better to endure patiently a smart which nobody feels but yourself, than to commit a hasty action whose evil consequences will extend to all connected with you— and, besides, the Bible bids us return good for evil."

---

2. **Rasselas** *The History of Rasselas, Prince of Abyssinia*, a moralizing novel by Samuel Johnson.

"But then it seems disgraceful to be flogged, and to be sent to stand in the middle of a room full of people; and you are such a great girl: I am far younger than you, and I could not bear it."

"Yet it would be your duty to bear it, if you could not avoid it: it is weak and silly to say you *cannot bear* what it is your fate to be required to bear."

I heard her with wonder: I could not comprehend this doctrine of endurance; and still less could I understand or sympathize with the forbearance she expressed for her chastiser. Still I felt that Helen Burns considered things by a light invisible to my eyes. I suspected she might be right and I wrong; but I would not ponder the matter deeply: like Felix,[3] I put it off to a more convenient season.

"You say you have faults, Helen: what are they? To me you seem very good."

"Then learn from me, not to judge by appearances: I am, as Miss Scatcherd said, slatternly; I seldom put, and never keep, things in order; I am careless; I forget rules; I read when I should learn my lessons; I have no method; and sometimes I say, like you, I cannot *bear* to be subjected to systematic arrangements. This is all very provoking to Miss Scatcherd, who is naturally neat, punctual, and particular."

"And cross and cruel," I added; but Helen Burns would not admit my addition: she kept silence.

"Is Miss Temple as severe to you as Miss Scatcherd?"

At the utterance of Miss Temple's name, a soft smile flitted over her grave face.

"Miss Temple is full of goodness; it pains her to be severe to anyone, even the worst in the school: she sees my errors, and tells me of them gently; and, if I do anything worthy of praise, she gives me my meed liberally. One strong proof of my wretchedly defective nature is that even her expostulations, so mild, so rational, have not influence to cure me of my faults; and even her praise, though I value it most highly, cannot stimulate me to continued care and foresight."

"That is curious," said I: "it is so easy to be careful."

"For *you* I have no doubt it is. I observed you in your class this morning, and saw you were closely attentive: your thoughts never seemed to wander while

---

3. Felix in the Bible, governor of Judea who released Paul from prison and deferred his trial until a more "convenient season" (Acts 24:25).

TAKE NOTES

Miss Miller explained the lesson and questioned you. Now, mine continually rove away: when I should be listening to Miss Scatcherd, and collecting all she says with assiduity,[4] often I lose the very sound of her voice; I fall into a sort of dream. Sometimes I think I am in Northumberland, and that the noises I hear round me are the bubbling of a little brook which runs through Deepden, near our house;—then, when it comes to my turn to reply, I have to be wakened; and, having heard nothing of what was read for listening to the visionary brook, I have no answer ready."

"Yet how well you replied this afternoon."

"It was mere chance: the subject on which we had been reading had interested me. This afternoon, instead of dreaming of Deepden, I was wondering how a man who wished to do right could act so unjustly and unwisely as Charles the First sometimes did; and I thought what a pity it was that, with his integrity and conscientiousness, he could see no farther than the prerogatives of the crown. If he had but been able to look to a distance, and see how what they call the spirit of the age was tending! Still, I like Charles—I respect him—I pity him, poor murdered king! Yes, his enemies were the worst: they shed blood they had no right to shed. How dared they kill him!"

Helen was talking to herself now: she had forgotten I could not very well understand her—that I was ignorant, or nearly so, of the subject she discussed. I recalled her to my level.

"And when Miss Temple teaches you, do your thoughts wander then?"

"No, certainly, not often; because Miss Temple has generally something to say which is newer to me than my own reflections: her language is singularly agreeable to me, and the information she communicates is often just what I wished to gain."

"Well, then, with Miss Temple you are good?"

"Yes, in a passive way: I make no effort; I follow as inclination guides me. There is no merit in such goodness."

"A great deal: you are good to those who are good to you. It is all I ever desire to be. If people were always

---

4. assiduity (as′ ə dyōō′ ə tē) *n.* constant care and attention; diligence.

kind and obedient to those who are cruel and unjust, the wicked people would have it all their own way: they would never feel afraid, and so they would never alter, but would grow worse and worse. When we are struck at without a reason, we should strike back again very hard; I am sure we should—so hard as to teach the person who struck us never to do it again."

"You will change your mind, I hope, when you grow older: as yet you are but a little untaught girl."

"But I feel this, Helen: I must dislike those who, whatever I do to please them, persist in disliking me; I must resist those who punish me unjustly. It is as natural as that I should love those who show me affection, or submit to punishment when I feel it is deserved."

"... Love your enemies; bless them that curse you; do good to them that hate you and despitefully use you."

"Then I should love Mrs. Reed, which I cannot do; I should bless her son John, which is impossible."

In her turn, Helen Burns asked me to explain; and I proceeded forthwith to pour out, in my way, the tale of my sufferings and resentments. Bitter and truculent when excited, I spoke as I felt, without reserve or softening.

Helen heard me patiently to the end: I expected she would then make a remark, but she said nothing.

"Well," I asked impatiently, "is not Mrs. Reed a hard-hearted, bad woman?"

"She has been unkind to you, no doubt; because, you see, she dislikes your cast of character, as Miss Scatcherd does mine: but how minutely you remember all she has done and said to you! What a singularly deep impression her injustice seems to have made on your heart! No ill usage so brands its record on my feelings. Would you not be happier if you tried to forget her severity, together with the passionate emotions it excited? Life appears to me too short to be spent in nursing animosity or registering wrongs. We are, and must be, one and all, burdened with faults in this world: but the time will soon come when, I trust, we shall put them off in putting off our corruptible bodies; when debasement and sin will fall from us with this cumbrous frame of flesh, and only the spark of the spirit will remain,—the impalpable principle of life and

TAKE NOTES

thought, pure as when it left the Creator to inspire the creature: whence[5] it came it will return; perhaps again to be communicated to some being higher than man— perhaps to pass through gradations of glory, from the pale human soul to brighten to the seraph![6] Surely it will never, on the contrary, be suffered to degenerate from man to fiend? No; I cannot believe that: I hold another creed; which no one ever taught me, and which I seldom mention; but in which I delight, and to which I cling: for it extends hope to all: it makes Eternity a rest—a mighty home, not a terror and abyss. Besides, with this creed, I can so clearly distinguish between the criminal and his crime; I can so sincerely forgive the first while I abhor the last: with this creed revenge never worries my heart, degradation never too deeply disgusts me, injustice never crushes me too low: I live in calm, looking to the end."

Helen's head, always drooping, sank a little lower as she finished this sentence. I saw by her look she wished no longer to talk to me, but rather to converse with her own thoughts. She was not allowed much time for meditation: a monitor, a great rough girl, presently came up, exclaiming in a strong Cumberland accent—

"Helen Burns, if you don't go and put your drawer in order, and fold up your work this minute, I'll tell Miss Scatcherd to come and look at it!"

Helen sighed as her reverie fled, and getting up, obeyed the monitor without reply as without delay.

---

5. **whence** the place from which.
6. **seraph** angel of the highest order.

Dover Beach

by Matthew Arnold

The sea is calm tonight.
The tide is full, the moon lies fair
Upon the straits;[1] on the French coast the light
Gleams and is gone; the cliffs of England stand,
5   Glimmering and vast, out in the tranquil bay.
Come to the window, sweet is the night air!

Only, from the long line of spray
Where the sea meets the moon-blanched land,
Listen! you hear the grating roar
10   Of pebbles which the waves draw back, and fling,
At their return, up the high strand,[2]
Begin, and cease, and then again begin,
With tremulous cadence slow, and bring
The eternal note of sadness in.
15   Sophocles[3] long ago
Heard it on the Aegean,[4] and it brought
Into his mind the turbid ebb and flow
Of human misery; we
Find also in the sound a thought,
20   Hearing it by this distant northern sea.

The Sea of Faith
Was once, too, at the full, and round earth's shore
Lay like the folds of a bright girdle furled.
But now I only hear
25   Its melancholy, long, withdrawing roar,
Retreating, to the breath
Of the night wind, down the vast edges drear
And naked shingles[5] of the world.

---

1. **straits** Straits of Dover, between England and France.
2. **strand** shore.
3. **Sophocles** (säf´ ə klēz´) Greek tragic dramatist (496?–406 b.c.).
4. **Aegean** (ē jē´ ən) arm of the Mediterranean Sea between Greece and Turkey.
5. **shingles** *n.* beaches covered with large, coarse, waterworn gravel.

TAKE NOTES

Ah, love, let us be true
30 To one another! for the world, which seems
To lie before us like a land of dreams,
So various, so beautiful, so new,
Hath really neither joy, nor love, nor light,
Nor certitude, nor peace, nor help for pain;
35 And we are here as on a darkling[6] plain
Swept with confused alarms of struggle and flight,
Where ignorant armies clash by night.

---

6. **darkling** *adj.* in the dark.

Recessional[1]

by Rudyard Kipling

BACKGROUND *In 1897, a national celebration called the "Diamond Jubilee" was held in honor of the sixtieth anniversary of Queen Victoria's reign. The occasion prompted a great deal of boasting about the strength and greatness of the empire. Kipling responded to the celebration by writing this poem, reminding the people of England that the British empire might not last forever.*

God of our fathers, known of old—
    Lord of our far-flung battle-line—
Beneath whose awful Hand we hold
    Dominion over palm and pine—
5 Lord God of Hosts, be with us yet
Lest we forget—lest we forget!

The tumult and the shouting dies—
    The Captains and the Kings depart—
Still stands Thine ancient Sacrifice,
10   An humble and a contrite heart.[2]
Lord God of Hosts, be with us yet,
Lest we forget—lest we forget!

Far-called, our navies melt away—
    On dune and headland sinks the fire[3]—
15 Lo, all our pomp of yesterday
    Is one with Nineveh[4] and Tyre![5]
Judge of the Nations, spare us yet,
Lest we forget—lest we forget!

---

1. **Recessional** hymn sung at the end of a religious service.
2. **An . . . heart** allusion to the Bible (Psalms 51:17) "The sacrifices of God are a broken spirit: a broken and contrite heart, O God, thou wilt not despise."
3. **On . . . fire** Bonfires were lit on high ground all over Britain as part of the opening ceremonies of the Jubilee celebration.
4. **Nineveh** (nin´ ə və) ancient capital of the Assyrian Empire, the ruins of which were discovered buried in desert sands in the 1850s.
5. **Tyre** (tīr) once a great port and the center of ancient Phoenician culture, now a small town in Lebanon.

"

TAKE NOTES

____

____

____

____

____

____

____

____

____

____

____

____

____

____

____

____

____

____

____

____

____

____

If, drunk with sight of power, we loose

20   Wild tongues that have not Thee in awe—
Such boasting as the Gentiles use
  Or lesser breeds without the Law—[6]
Lord God of Hosts, be with us yet,
Lest we forget—lest we forget!

25 For heathen heart that puts her trust
  In reeking tube[7] and iron shard[8]—
All valiant dust that builds on dust,
  And guarding calls not Thee to guard—
For frantic boast and foolish word,
30 Thy mercy on Thy People, Lord!

---

6. **Such boasting . . . Law** allusion to the Bible (Romans 2:14) "For when the Gentiles, which have not the law, do by nature the things contained in the law, these, having not the law, are a law unto themselves."
7. **tube** barrel of a gun.
8. **shard** fragment of a bombshell.

The Widow at Windsor

by Rudyard Kipling

'Ave you 'eard o' the Widow at Windsor
    With a hairy gold crown on 'er 'ead?
She 'as ships on the foam—she 'as millions at 'ome,
    An' she pays us poor beggars in red.
5   (Ow, poor beggars in red!)
There's 'er nick on the cavalry 'orses,
    There's 'er mark on the medical stores—
An' 'er troops you'll find with a fair wind be'ind
    That takes us to various wars.
10   (Poor beggars!—barbarious wars!)
        Then 'ere's to the Widow at Windsor,
            An' 'ere's to the stores an' the guns,
        The men an' the 'orses what makes up the
            forces
            O' Missis Victorier's sons.
15   (Poor beggars! Victorier's sons!)

Walk wide o' the Widow at Windsor,
    For 'alf o' Creation she owns:
We'ave bought 'er the same with the sword an' the
    flame,
    An' we've salted it down with our bones.
20   (Poor beggars!—it's blue with our bones!)
Hands off o' the sons o' the widow,
    Hands off o' the goods in 'er shop.
For the kings must come down an' the emperors
    frown
    When the Widow at Windsor says "Stop!"
25   (Poor beggars!—we're sent to say "Stop!")
        Then 'ere's to the Lodge o' the Widow,
            From the Pole to the Tropics it
            runs—
         To the Lodge that we tile with the rank an'
            the file,
            An' open in form with the guns.
30   (Poor beggars!—it's always they guns!)

TAKE NOTES

We 'ave 'eard o' the Widow at Windsor,
   It's safest to leave 'er alone:
For 'er sentries we stand by the sea an' the land
   Wherever the bugles are blown.
35   (Poor beggars!—an' don't we get blown!)
   Take 'old o' the Wings o' the Mornin',
   An' flop round the earth till you're dead;
But you won't get away from the tune that they play
   To the bloomin' old rag over'ead.
40   (Poor beggars!—it's 'ot over'ead!)
   Then 'ere's to the sons o' the Widow,
     Wherever, 'owever they roam.
   'Ere's all they desire, an' if they require
     A speedy return to their 'ome.
45   (Poor beggars!—they'll never see 'ome!)

God's Grandeur

by Gerald Manley Hopkins

BACKGROUND *Surprisingly, when Gerard Manley Hopkins died, none of his obituaries mentioned that he was a poet and only a few friends were aware of this fact. One of these friends was Robert Bridges, an Oxford classmate and later the British poet laureate. Bridges had corresponded with Hopkins and took an interest in his experiments with rhythm. It was through Bridges's efforts that a volume of Hopkins's poetry was published for the first time in 1918. Today, Bridges is little known, but his once-obscure friend Gerard Manley Hopkins is a famous Victorian poet.*

The world is charged with the grandeur of God.
    It will flame out, like shining from shook foil;[1]
    It gathers to a greatness, like the ooze of oil
Crushed.[2] Why do men then now not reck his rod?[3]
5 Generations have trod, have trod, have trod;
    And all is seared with trade; bleared, smeared
      with toil;
    And wears man's smudge and shares man's
      smell: the soil
Is bare now, nor can foot feel, being shod.

And for all this, nature is never spent;
10   There lives the dearest freshness deep down
      things;
And though the last lights off the black West went
    Oh, morning, at the brown brink eastward,
      springs—
Because the Holy Ghost over the bent
    World broods with warm breast and with ah!
      bright wings.

---

1. **foil** *n.* tinsel.
2. **crushed** squeezed from olives.
3. **reck his rod** heed God's authority.

Spring and Fall:
to a Young Child

by Gerald Manley Hopkins

Márgarét, áre you gríeving
Over Goldengrove unleaving?
Leáves, líke the things of man, you
With your fresh thoughts care for, can you?
5 Áh! ás the heart grows older
It will come to such sights colder
By and by, nor spare a sigh
Though worlds of wanwood[1] leafmeal[2] lie;
And yet you wíll weep and know why.
10 Now no matter, child, the name:
Sórrow's spríngs áre the same.
Nor mouth had, no nor mind, expressed
What heart heard of, ghost[3] guessed:
It ís the blight man was born for,
15 It is Margaret you mourn for.

---

1. **wanwood** (wän' wood) pale wood.
2. **leafmeal** ground-up decomposed leaves.
3. **ghost** spirit.

To an Athlete Dying Young

by A. E. Housman

The time you won your town the race
We chaired you through the marketplace;
Man and boy stood cheering by,
And home we brought you shoulder-high.

5 Today, the road all runners come,
Shoulder-high we bring you home,
And set you at your threshold down,
Townsman of a stiller town.

Smart lad, to slip betimes away
10 From fields where glory does not stay
And early though the laurel[1] grows
It withers quicker than the rose.

Eyes the shady night has shut
Cannot see the record cut,
15 And silence sounds no worse than cheers
After earth has stopped the ears:

Now you will not swell the rout
Of lads that wore their honors out,
Runners whom renown outran
20 And the name died before the man.

So set, before its echoes fade,
The fleet foot on the sill of shade.
And hold to the low lintel up
The still-defended challenge cup.

25 And round that early-laureled head
Will flock to gaze the strengthless dead,
And find unwithered on its curls
The garland briefer than a girl's.

---

1. **laurel** symbol of victory.

When I Was One-and-Twenty

by A. E. Housman

When I was one-and-twenty
   I heard a wise man say,
"Give crowns and pounds and guineas[1]
   But not your heart away;
5 Give pearls away and rubies
   But keep your fancy free."
But I was one-and-twenty,
   No use to talk to me.

When I was one-and-twenty
10   I heard him say again,
"The heart out of the bosom
   Was never given in vain;
'Tis paid with sighs a plenty
   And sold for endless rue."
15 And I am two-and-twenty,
   And oh, 'tis true, 'tis true.

---

1. **crowns . . . guineas** denominations of money.

Sailing to Byzantium

by William Butler Yeats

I

That is no country for old men. The young
In one another's arms, birds in the trees
—Those dying generations—at their song,
The salmon-falls, the mackerel-crowded seas,
5 Fish, flesh, or fowl, commend all summer long
Whatever is begotten, born, and dies.
Caught in that sensual music all neglect
Monuments of unaging intellect.

II

An aged man is but a paltry thing,
10 A tattered coat upon a stick, unless
Soul clap its hands and sing, and louder sing
For every tatter in its mortal dress,
Nor is there singing school but studying
Monuments of its own magnificence;
15 And therefore I have sailed the seas and come
To the holy city of Byzantium.[1]

III

O sages standing in God's holy fire
As in the gold mosaic of a wall,[2]
Come from the holy fire, perne in a gyre,[3]
20 And be the singing-masters of my soul.
Consume my heart away; sick with desire
And fastened to a dying animal
It knows not what it is; and gather me
Into the artifice of eternity.

---

1. **Byzantium** (bi zan´ shē əm) ancient capital of the Eastern Roman (or Byzantine) Empire and the seat of the Greek Orthodox Church; today, Istanbul, Turkey. For Yeats, Byzantium symbolized the world of art as opposed to the world of time and nature.
2. **sages . . . wall** wise men portrayed in mosaic on the walls of Byzantine churches.
3. **perne . . . gyre** spin in a spiraling motion.

TAKE NOTES

IV

25 Once out of nature I shall never take
My bodily form from any natural thing,
But such a form as Grecian goldsmiths make
Of hammered gold and gold enameling
To keep a drowsy Emperor awake;
30 Or set upon a golden bough to sing[4]
To lords and ladies of Byzantium
Of what is past, or passing, or to come.

---

4. To . . . sing Yeats wrote, "I have read somewhere that in the Emperor's palace at Byzantium was a tree made of gold and silver, and artificial birds that sang."

The Rocking-Horse Winner

by D. H. Lawrence

BACKGROUND *During the first half of the twentieth century, Britain had a rigid class structure. Its upper classes tried to live at the "right" addresses, attend the "right" schools, and have the "right" friends. In "The Rocking-Horse Winner," Paul's mother is desperate to maintain upper-class appearances despite her husband's "small income."*

There was a woman who was beautiful, who started with all the advantages, yet she had no luck. She married for love, and the love turned to dust. She had bonny children, yet she felt they had been thrust upon her, and she could not love them. They looked at her coldly, as if they were finding fault with her. And hurriedly she felt she must cover up some fault in herself. Yet what it was that she must cover up she never knew. Nevertheless, when her children were present, she always felt the center of her heart go hard. This troubled her, and in her manner she was all the more gentle and anxious for her children, as if she loved them very much. Only she herself knew that at the center of her heart was a hard little place that could not feel love, no, not for anybody. Everybody else said of her: "She is such a good mother. She adores her children." Only she herself, and her children themselves, knew it was not so. They read it in each other's eyes.

There were a boy and two little girls. They lived in a pleasant house, with a garden and they had discreet servants, and felt themselves superior to anyone in the neighborhood.

Although they lived in style, they felt always an anxiety in the house. There was never enough money.

TAKE NOTES

TAKE NOTES

The mother had a small income and the father had a small income, but not nearly enough for the social position which they had to keep up. The father went into town to some office. But though he had good prospects, these prospects never materialized. There was always the grinding sense of the shortage of money, though the style was always kept up.

At last the mother said, "I will see if *I* can't make something." But she did not know where to begin. She racked her brains, and tried this thing and the other, but could not find anything successful. The failure made deep lines come into her face. Her children were growing up, they would have to go to school. There must be more money, there must be more money. The father, who was always very handsome and expensive in his tastes, seemed as if he never *would* be able to do anything worth doing. And the mother, who had a great belief in herself, did not succeed any better, and her tastes were just as expensive.

And so the house came to be haunted by the unspoken phrase: *There must be more money! There must be more money!* The children could hear it all the time, though nobody said it aloud. They heard it at Christmas, when the expensive and splendid toys filled the nursery. Behind the shining modern rocking horse, behind the smart doll's house, a voice would start whispering: "There *must* be more money! There *must* be more money!" And the children would stop playing, to listen for a moment. They would look into each other's eyes to see if they had all heard. And each one saw in the eyes of the other two that they too had heard. "There *must* be more money! There *must* be more money!"

It came whispering from the springs of the still-swaying rocking horse, and even the horse, bending his wooden, champing head, heard it. The big doll, sitting so pink and smirking in her new pram,[1] could hear it quite plainly, and seemed to be smirking all the more self-consciously because of it. The foolish puppy, too, that took the place of the teddy bear, he was looking so extraordinarily foolish for no other reason but that he heard the secret whisper all over the house: "There *must* be more money."

---

1. **pram** baby carriage.

Yet nobody ever said it aloud. The whisper was everywhere, and therefore no one spoke it. Just as no one ever says: "We are breathing!" in spite of the fact that breath is coming and going all the time.

"Mother!" said the boy Paul one day. "Why don't we keep a car of our own? Why do we always use uncle's, or else a taxi?"

"Because we're the poor members of the family," said the mother.

"But why *are* we, mother?"

"Well—I suppose," she said slowly and bitterly, "it's because your father has no luck."

The boy was silent for some time.

"Is luck money, mother?" he asked, rather timidly.

"No, Paul! Not quite. It's what causes you to have money."

"Oh!" said Paul vaguely. "I thought when Uncle Oscar said *filthy lucker,* it meant money."

"*Filthy lucre* does mean money," said the mother. "But it's lucre, not luck."

"Oh!" said the boy. "Then what *is* luck, mother?"

"It's what causes you to have money. If you're lucky you have money. That's why it's better to be born lucky than rich. If you're rich, you may lose your money. But if you're lucky, you will always get more money."

"Oh! Will you! And is father not lucky?"

"Very unlucky, I should say," she said bitterly.

The boy watched her with unsure eyes.

"Why?" he asked.

"I don't know. Nobody ever knows why one person is lucky and another unlucky."

"Don't they? Nobody at all? Does *nobody* know?"

"Perhaps God! But He never tells."

"He ought to, then. And aren't you lucky either, mother?"

"I can't be, if I married an unlucky husband."

"But by yourself, aren't you?"

"I used to think I was, before I married. Now I think I am very unlucky indeed."

"Why?"

"Well—never mind! Perhaps I'm not really," she said.

The child looked at her, to see if she meant it. But he saw, by the lines of her mouth, that she was only trying to hide something from him.

TAKE NOTES

"Well, anyhow," he said stoutly, "I'm a lucky person."

"Why?" said his mother, with a sudden laugh.

He stared at her. He didn't even know why he had said it.

"God told me," he asserted, brazening[2] it out.

"I hope He did, dear!" she said, again with a laugh, but rather bitter.

"He did, mother!"

"Excellent!" said the mother, using one of her husband's exclamations.

The boy saw she did not believe him; or rather, that she paid no attention to his assertion. This angered him somewhere, and made him want to compel her attention.

He went off by himself, vaguely, in a childish way, seeking for the clue to "luck." Absorbed, taking no heed of other people, he went about with a sort of stealth, seeking inwardly for luck. He wanted luck, he wanted it, he wanted it. When the two girls were playing dolls, in the nursery, he would sit on his big rocking horse, charging madly into space, with a frenzy that made the little girls peer at him uneasily. Wildly the horse careered, the waving dark hair of the boy tossed, his eyes had a strange glare in them. The little girls dared not speak to him.

When he had ridden to the end of his mad little journey, he climbed down and stood in front of his rocking horse, staring fixedly into its lowered face. Its red mouth was slightly open, its big eye was wide and glassy bright.

"Now!" he would silently command the snorting steed. "Now take me to where there is luck! Now take me!"

And he would slash the horse on the neck with the little whip he had asked Uncle Oscar for. He *knew* the horse could take him to where there was luck, if only he forced it. So he would mount again, and start on his furious ride, hoping at last to get there. He knew he could get there.

"You'll break your horse, Paul!" said the nurse.

"He's always riding like that! I wish he'd leave off!" said his elder sister Joan.

---

2. **brazening** (brā′ zən iŋ) *v.* daring boldly or shamelessly.

But he only glared down on them in silence. Nurse gave him up. She could make nothing of him. Anyhow he was growing beyond her.

One day his mother and his Uncle Oscar came in when he was on one of his furious rides. He did not speak to them.

"Hallo! you young jockey! Riding a winner?" said his uncle.

"Aren't you growing too big for a rocking horse? You're not a very little boy any longer, you know," said his mother.

But Paul only gave a blue glare from his big, rather close-set eyes. He would speak to nobody when he was in full tilt. His mother watched him with an anxious expression on her face.

At last he suddenly stopped forcing his horse into the mechanical gallop, and slid down.

"Well, I got there!" he announced fiercely, his blue eyes still flaring, and his sturdy long legs straddling apart.

"Where did you get to?" asked his mother.

"Where I wanted to go to," he flared back at her.

"That's right, son!" said Uncle Oscar. "Don't you stop till you get there. What's the horse's name?"

"He doesn't have a name," said the boy.

"Gets on without all right?" asked the uncle.

"Well, he has different names. He was called Sansovino last week."

"Sansovino, eh? Won the Ascot.[3] How did you know his name?"

"He always talks about horse races with Bassett," said Joan.

The uncle was delighted to find that his small nephew was posted with all the racing news. Bassett, the young gardener who had been wounded in the left foot in the war, and had got his present job through Oscar Cresswell, whose batman[4] he had been, was a perfect blade of the "turf."[5] He lived in the racing events, and the small boy lived with him.

Oscar Cresswell got it all from Bassett.

"Master Paul comes and asks me, so I can't do

---

3. Ascot major English horse race.
4. batman British military officer's orderly.
5. blade . . . "turf" horse-racing fan.

TAKE NOTES

more than tell him, sir," said Bassett, his face terribly serious, as if he were speaking of religious matters.

"And does he ever put anything on a horse he fancies?"

"Well—I don't want to give him away—he's a young sport, a fine sport, sir. Would you mind asking him yourself? He sort of takes a pleasure in it, and perhaps he'd feel I was giving him away, sir, if you don't mind."

Bassett was serious as a church.

The uncle went back to his nephew, and took him off for a ride in the car.

"Say, Paul, old man, do you ever put anything on a horse?" the uncle asked.

The boy watched the handsome man closely.

"Why, do you think I oughtn't to?" he parried.

"Not a bit of it! I thought perhaps you might give me a tip for the Lincoln."[6]

The car sped on into the country, going down to Uncle Oscar's place in Hampshire.

"Honor bright?" said the nephew.

"Honor bright, son!" said the uncle.

"Well, then, Daffodil."

"Daffodil! I doubt it, sonny. What about Mirza?"

"I only know the winner," said the boy. "That's Daffodil!"

"Daffodil, eh?"

There was a pause. Daffodil was an obscure horse comparatively.

"Uncle!"

"Yes, son?"

"You won't let it go any further, will you? I promised Bassett."

"Bassett be hanged, old man! What's he got to do with it?"

"We're partners! We've been partners from the first! Uncle, he lent me my first five shillings, which I lost. I promised him, honor bright, it was only between me and him: only you gave me that ten-shilling note I started winning with, so I thought you were lucky. You won't let it go any further, will you?"

The boy gazed at his uncle from those big, hot, blue eyes, set rather close together. The uncle stirred and laughed uneasily.

---

6. **Lincoln** major English horse race.

"Right you are, son! I'll keep your tip private. Daffodil, eh! How much are you putting on him?"

"All except twenty pounds," said the boy. "I keep that in reserve."

The uncle thought it a good joke.

"You keep twenty pounds in reserve, do you, you young romancer? What are you betting, then?"

"I'm betting three hundred," said the boy gravely. "But it's between you and me, Uncle Oscar! Honor bright?"

The uncle burst into a roar of laughter.

"It's between you and me all right, you young Nat Gould,"[7] he said, laughing. "But where's your three hundred?"

"Bassett keeps it for me. We're partners."

"You are, are you! And what is Bassett putting on Daffodil?"

"He won't go quite as high as I do, I expect. Perhaps he'll go a hundred and fifty."

"What, pennies?" laughed the uncle.

"Pounds," said the child, with a surprised look at his uncle. "Bassett keeps a bigger reserve than I do."

Between wonder and amusement, Uncle Oscar was silent. He pursued the matter no further, but he determined to take his nephew with him to the Lincoln races.

"Now, son," he said, "I'm putting twenty on Mirza, and I'll put five for you on any horse you fancy. What's your pick?"

"Daffodil, uncle!"

"No, not the fiver on Daffodil!"

"I should if it was my own five," said the child.

"Good! Good! Right you are! A fiver for me and a fiver for you on Daffodil."

The child had never been to a race meeting before, and his eyes were blue fire. He pursed his mouth tight, and watched. A Frenchman just in front had put his money on Lancelot. Wild with excitement, he flayed his arms up and down, yelling *"Lancelot! Lancelot!"* in his French accent.

Daffodil came in first, Lancelot second, Mirza third. The child, flushed and with eyes blazing, was curiously

---

7. Nat Gould famous English sportswriter and authority on horse racing.

TAKE NOTES

serene. His uncle brought him five five-pound notes: four to one.

"What am I to do with these?" he cried, waving them before the boy's eyes.

"I suppose we'll talk to Bassett," said the boy. "I expect I have fifteen hundred now; and twenty in reserve; and this twenty."

His uncle studied him for some moments.

"Look here, son!" he said. "You're not serious about Bassett and that fifteen hundred, are you?"

"Yes, I am. But it's between you and me, uncle! Honor bright!"

"Honor bright all right, son! But I must talk to Bassett."

"If you'd like to be a partner, uncle, with Bassett and me, we could all be partners. Only you'd have to promise, honor bright, uncle, not to let it go beyond us three. Bassett and I are lucky, and you must be lucky, because it was your ten shillings I started winning with. . . ."

Uncle Oscar took both Bassett and Paul into Richmond Park for an afternoon, and there they talked.

"It's like this, you see, sir," Bassett said. "Master Paul would get me talking about racing events, spinning yarns, you know, sir. And he was always keen on knowing if I'd made or if I'd lost. It's about a year since, now, that I put five shillings on Blush of Dawn for him—and we lost. Then the luck turned, with that ten shillings he had from you, that we put on Singhalese. And since that time, it's been pretty steady, all things considering. What do you say, Master Paul?"

"We're all right when we're *sure,*" said Paul. "It's when we're not quite sure that we go down."

"Oh, but we're careful then," said Bassett.

"But when are you *sure?*" smiled Uncle Oscar.

"It's Master Paul, sir," said Bassett, in a secret, religious voice. "It's as if he had it from heaven. Like Daffodil now, for the Lincoln. That was as sure as eggs."

"Did you put anything on Daffodil?" asked Oscar Cresswell.

"Yes, sir. I made my bit."

"And my nephew?"

Bassett was obstinately silent, looking at Paul.

"I made twelve hundred, didn't I, Bassett? I told uncle I was putting three hundred on Daffodil."

"That's right," said Bassett, nodding.

"But where's the money?" asked the uncle.

"I keep it safe locked up, sir. Master Paul, he can have it any minute he likes to ask for it."

"What, fifteen hundred pounds?"

"And twenty! And *forty,* that is, with the twenty he made on the course."

"It's amazing!" said the uncle.

"If Master Paul offers you to be partners, sir, I would, if I were you; if you'll excuse me," said Bassett.

Oscar Cresswell thought about it.

"I'll see the money," he said.

They drove home again, and sure enough, Bassett came round to the garden house with fifteen hundred pounds in notes. The twenty pounds reserve was left with Joe Glee, in the Turf Commission deposit.

"You see, it's all right, uncle, when I'm *sure!* Then we go strong, for all we're worth. Don't we, Bassett?"

"We do that, Master Paul."

"And when are you sure?" said the uncle, laughing.

"Oh, well, sometimes I'm *absolutely* sure, like about Daffodil," said the boy, "and sometimes I have an idea; and sometimes I haven't even an idea, have I, Bassett? Then we're careful, because we mostly go down."

"You do, do you! And when you're sure, like about Daffodil, what makes you sure, sonny?"

"Oh, well, I don't know," said the boy uneasily. "I'm sure, you know, uncle; that's all."

"It's as if he had it from heaven, sir," Bassett reiterated.

"I should say so!" said the uncle.

But he became a partner. And when the Leger was coming on, Paul was "sure" about Lively Spark, which was a quite inconsiderable horse. The boy insisted on putting a thousand on the horse, Bassett went for five hundred, and Oscar Cresswell two hundred. Lively Spark came in first, and the betting had been ten to one against him. Paul had made ten thousand.

"You see," he said. "I was absolutely sure of him."

Even Oscar Cresswell had cleared two thousand.

"Look here, son," he said, "this sort of thing makes me nervous."

TAKE NOTES

TAKE NOTES

"It needn't, uncle! Perhaps I shan't be sure again for a long time."

"But what are you going to do with your money?" asked the uncle.

"Of course," said the boy, "I started it for mother. She said she had no luck, because father is unlucky, so I thought if *I* was lucky, it might stop whispering."

"What might stop whispering?"

"Our house! I *hate* our house for whispering."

"What does it whisper?"

"Why—why"—the boy fidgeted—"why, I don't know! But it's always short of money, you know, uncle."

"I know it, son, I know it."

"You know people send mother writs, don't you, uncle?"

"I'm afraid I do," said the uncle.

"And then the house whispers like people laughing at you behind your back. It's awful, that is! I thought if I was lucky . . ."

"You might stop it," added the uncle.

The boy watched him with big blue eyes, that had an uncanny cold fire in them, and he said never a word.

"Well then!" said the uncle. "What are we doing?"

"I shouldn't like mother to know I was lucky," said the boy.

"Why not, son?"

"She'd stop me."

"I don't think she would."

"Oh!"—and the boy writhed in an odd way—"I *don't* want her to know, uncle."

"All right, son! We'll manage it without her knowing."

They managed it very easily. Paul, at the other's suggestion, handed over five thousand pounds to his uncle, who deposited it with the family lawyer, who was then to inform Paul's mother that a relative had put five thousand pounds into his hands, which sum was to be paid out a thousand pounds at a time, on the mother's birthday, for the next five years.

"So she'll have a birthday present of a thousand pounds for five successive years," said Uncle Oscar. "I hope it won't make it all the harder for her later."

Paul's mother had her birthday in November. The house had been "whispering" worse than ever lately, and even in spite of his luck, Paul could not bear up against it. He was very anxious to see the effect of the birthday letter, telling his mother about the thousand pounds.

When there were no visitors, Paul now took his meals with his parents, as he was beyond the nursery control. His mother went into town nearly every day. She had discovered that she had an odd knack of sketching furs and dress materials, so she worked secretly in the studio of a friend who was the chief "artist" for the leading drapers. She drew the figures of ladies in furs and ladies in silk and sequins for the newspaper advertisements. This young woman artist earned several thousand pounds a year, but Paul's mother only made several hundreds, and she was again dissatisfied. She so wanted to be first in something, and she did not succeed, even in making sketches for drapery advertisements.

She was down to breakfast on the morning of her birthday. Paul watched her face as she read her letters. He knew the lawyer's letter. As his mother read it, her face hardened and became more expressionless. Then a cold, determined look came on her mouth. She hid the letter under the pile of others, and said not a word about it.

"Didn't you have anything nice in the post for your birthday, mother?" said Paul.

"Quite moderately nice," she said, her voice cold and absent.

She went away to town without saying more.

But in the afternoon Uncle Oscar appeared. He said Paul's mother had had a long interview with the lawyer, asking if the whole five thousand could not be advanced at once, as she was in debt.

"What do you think, uncle?" said the boy.

"I leave it to you, son."

"Oh, let her have it, then! We can get some more with the other," said the boy.

"A bird in the hand is worth two in the bush, laddie!" said Uncle Oscar.

"But I'm sure to *know* for the Grand National; or the Lincolnshire; or else the Derby.[8] I'm sure to know for *one* of them," said Paul.

---

8. **Grand National . . . Derby** major English horse races.

TAKE NOTES

So Uncle Oscar signed the agreement, and Paul's mother touched the whole five thousand. Then something very curious happened. The voices in the house suddenly went mad, like a chorus of frogs on a spring evening. There were certain new furnishings, and Paul had a tutor. He was *really* going to Eton,[9] his father's school, in the following autumn. There were flowers in the winter, and a blossoming of the luxury Paul's mother had been used to. And yet the voices in the house, behind the sprays of mimosa and almond blossom, and from under the piles of iridescent cushions, simply trilled and screamed in a sort of ecstasy: "There *must* be more money! Oh-h-h! There *must* be more money! Oh, now, now-w! now-w-w— there *must* be more money!—more than ever! More than ever!"

It frightened Paul terribly. He studied away at his Latin and Greek with his tutors. But his intense hours were spent with Bassett. The Grand National had gone by: he had not "known," and had lost a hundred pounds. Summer was at hand. He was in agony for the Lincoln. But even for the Lincoln he didn't "know," and he lost fifty pounds. He became wild-eyed and strange, as if something were going to explode in him.

"Let it alone, son! Don't you bother about it!" urged Uncle Oscar. But it was as if the boy couldn't really hear what his uncle was saying.

"I've got to know for the Derby! I've *got* to know for the Derby!" the child reiterated, his big blue eyes blazing with a sort of madness.

His mother noticed how overwrought he was.

"You'd better go to the seaside. Wouldn't you like to go now to the seaside, instead of waiting? I think you'd better," she said, looking down at him anxiously, her heart curiously heavy because of him.

But the child lifted his uncanny blue eyes.

"I couldn't possibly go before the Derby, mother!" he said. "I couldn't possibly!"

"Why not?" she said, her voice becoming heavy when she was opposed. "Why not? You can still go from the seaside to see the Derby with your Uncle Oscar, if that's what you wish. No need for you to wait

---

9. **Eton** prestigious private school in England.

here. Besides, I think you care too much about these races. It's a bad sign. My family has been a gambling family, and you won't know till you grow up how much damage it has done. But it has done damage. I shall have to send Bassett away, and ask Uncle Oscar not to talk racing to you, unless you promise to be reasonable about it; go away to the seaside and forget it. You're all nerves!"

"I'll do what you like, mother, so long as you don't send me away till after the Derby," the boy said.

"Send you away from where? Just from this house?"

"Yes," he said, gazing at her.

"Why, you curious child, what makes you care about this house so much, suddenly? I never knew you loved it!"

He gazed at her without speaking. He had a secret within a secret, something he had not divulged, even to Bassctt or to his Unclc Oscar.

But his mother, after standing undecided and a little bit sullen for some moments, said:

"Very well, then! Don't go to the seaside till after the Derby, if you don't wish it. But promise me you won't let your nerves go to pieces! Promise you won't think so much about horse racing and *events,* as you call them!"

"Oh, no!" said the boy, casually. "I won't think much about them, mother. You needn't worry. I wouldn't worry, mother, if I were you."

"If you were me and I were you," said his mother, "I wonder what we should do!"

"But you know you needn't worry, mother, don't you?" the boy repeated.

"I should be awfully glad to know it," she said wearily.

"Oh, well, you *can,* you know. I mean you *ought* to know you needn't worry!" he insisted.

"Ought I? Then I'll see about it," she said.

Paul's secret of secrets was his wooden horse, that which had no name. Since he was emancipated from a nurse and a nursery governess, he had had his rocking horse removed to his own bedroom at the top of the house.

"Surely you're too big for a rocking horse!" his mother had remonstrated.

"Well, you see, mother, till I can have a *real* horse, I like to have *some* sort of animal about," had been his quaint answer.

TAKE NOTES

"Do you feel he keeps you company?" she laughed.

"Oh, yes! He's very good, he always keeps me company, when I'm there," said Paul.

So the horse, rather shabby, stood in an arrested prance in the boy's bedroom.

The Derby was drawing near, and the boy grew more and more tense. He hardly heard what was spoken to him, he was very frail, and his eyes were really uncanny. His mother had sudden strange seizures of uneasiness about him. Sometimes, for half an hour, she would feel a sudden anxiety about him that was almost anguish. She wanted to rush to him at once, and know he was safe.

Two nights before the Derby, she was at a big party in town, when one of her rushes of anxiety about her boy, her firstborn, gripped her heart till she could hardly speak. She fought with the feeling, might and main, for she believed in common sense. But it was too strong. She had to leave the dance and go downstairs to telephone to the country. The children's nursery governess was terribly surprised and startled at being rung up in the night.

"Are the children all right, Miss Wilmot?"

"Oh yes, they are quite all right."

"Master Paul? Is he all right?"

"He went to bed as right as a trivet.[10] Shall I run up and look at him?"

"No!" said Paul's mother reluctantly. "No! Don't trouble. It's all right. Don't sit up. We shall be home fairly soon." She did not want her son's privacy intruded upon.

"Very good," said the governess.

It was about one o'clock when Paul's mother and father drove up to their house. All was still. Paul's mother went to her room and slipped off her white fur cloak. She had told her maid not to wait up for her. She heard her husband downstairs, mixing a whisky-and-soda.

And then, because of the strange anxiety at her heart, she stole upstairs to her son's room. Noiselessly she went along the upper corridor. Was there a faint noise? What was it?

She stood, with arrested muscles, outside his door, listening. There was a strange, heavy, and yet not loud

---

10. **right as a trivet** perfectly right.

noise. Her heart stood still. It was a soundless noise, yet rushing and powerful. Something huge, in violent, hushed motion. What was it? What in God's name was it? She ought to know. She felt that she *knew* the noise. She knew what it was.

Yet she could not place it. She couldn't say what it was. And on and on it went, like madness.

Softly, frozen with anxiety and fear, she turned the door handle.

The room was dark. Yet in the space near the window, she heard and saw something plunging to and fro. She gazed in fear and amazement.

Then suddenly she switched on the light, and saw her son, in his green pajamas, madly surging on his rocking horse. The blaze of light suddenly lit him up, as he urged the wooden horse, and lit her up, as she stood, blond, in her dress of pale green and crystal, in the doorway.

"Paul!" she cried. "Whatever are you doing?"

"It's Malabar!" he screamed, in a powerful, strange voice. "It's Malabar!"

His eyes blazed at her for one strange and senseless second, as he ceased urging his wooden horse. Then he fell with a crash to the ground, and she, all her tormented motherhood flooding upon her, rushed to gather him up.

But he was unconscious, and unconscious he remained, with some brain fever. He talked and tossed, and his mother sat stonily by his side.

"Malabar! It's Malabar! Bassett, Bassett, I *know* it's Malabar!"

So the child cried, trying to get up and urge the rocking horse that gave him his inspiration.

"What does he mean by Malabar?" asked the heart-frozen mother.

"I don't know," said the father, stonily.

"What does he mean by Malabar?" she asked her brother Oscar.

"It's one of the horses running for the Derby," was the answer.

And, in spite of himself, Oscar Cresswell spoke to Bassett, and himself put a thousand on Malabar: at fourteen to one.

TAKE NOTES

The third day of the illness was critical: they were watching for a change. The boy, with his rather long, curly hair, was tossing ceaselessly on the pillow. He neither slept nor regained consciousness, and his eyes were like blue stones. His mother sat, feeling her heart had gone, turned actually into a stone.

In the evening, Oscar Cresswell did not come, but Bassett sent a message, saying could he come up for one moment, just one moment? Paul's mother was very angry at the intrusion, but on second thoughts she agreed. The boy was the same. Perhaps Bassett might bring him to consciousness.

The gardener, a shortish fellow with a little brown moustache and sharp little brown eyes, tiptoed into the room, touched his imaginary cap to Paul's mother, and stole to the bedside, staring with glittering, smallish eyes at the tossing, dying child.

"Master Paul!" he whispered. "Master Paul! Malabar came in first all right, a clean win. I did as you told me. You've made over seventy thousand pounds, you have; you've got over eighty thousand. Malabar came in all right, Master Paul."

"Malabar! Malabar! Did I say Malabar, mother? Did I say Malabar? Do you think I'm lucky, mother? I knew Malabar, didn't I? Over eighty thousand pounds! I call that lucky, don't you, mother? Over eighty thousand pounds! I knew, didn't I know I knew? Malabar came in all right. If I ride my horse till I'm sure, then I tell you, Bassett, you can go as high as you like. Did you go for all you were worth, Bassett?"

"I went a thousand on it, Master Paul."

"I never told you, mother, that if I can ride my horse, and *get there,* then I'm absolutely sure—oh, absolutely! Mother, did I ever tell you? I *am* lucky!"

"No, you never did," said the mother.

But the boy died in the night.

And even as he lay dead, his mother heard her brother's voice saying to her: "My God, Hester, you're eighty-odd thousand to the good, and a poor devil of a son to the bad. But, poor devil, poor devil, he's best gone out of a life where he rides his rocking horse to find a winner."

The Train from Rhodesia

by Nadine Gordimer

BACKGROUND *This story is set at a time when South Africa and Rhodesia (now Zimbabwe) enforced policies of racial separation, called* apartheid *in South Africa, ensuring the continued privileges of a white minority and its domination over the black majority.*

The train came out of the red horizon and bore down toward them over the single straight track. The stationmaster came out of his little brick station with its pointed chalet roof, feeling the creases in his serge uniform in his legs as well. A stir of preparedness rippled through the squatting native vendors waiting in the dust; the face of a carved wooden animal, eternally surprised, stuck out of a sack. The stationmaster's barefoot children wandered over. From the gray mud huts with the untidy heads that stood within a decorated mud wall, chickens, and dogs with their skin stretched like parchment over their bones, followed the piccanins[1] down to the track. The flushed and perspiring west cast a reflection, faint, without heat, upon the station, upon the tin shed marked "Goods," upon the walled kraal,[2] upon the gray tin house of the stationmaster and upon the sand, that lapped all around, from sky to sky, cast little rhythmical cups of shadow, so that the sand became the sea, and closed over the children's black feet softly and without imprint.

The stationmaster's wife sat behind the mesh of her veranda. Above her head the hunk of a sheep's carcass moved slightly, dangling in a current of air.

They waited.

The train called out, along the sky; but there was no answer; and the cry hung on: I'm coming . . . I'm coming . . .

---

1. **piccanins** *n.* native children.
2. **kraal** (kräl) *n.* fenced-in enclosure for cattle or sheep.

TAKE NOTES

The engine flared out now, big, whisking a dwindling body behind it; the track flared out to let it in.

Creaking, jerking, jostling, gasping, the train filled the station.

Here, let me see that one—the young woman curved her body farther out of the corridor window. Missus? smiled the old boy, looking at the creatures he held in his hand. From a piece of string on his gray finger hung a tiny woven basket; he lifted it, questioning. No, no, she urged, leaning down towards him, across the height of the train, towards the man in the piece of old rug; that one, that one, her hand commanded. It was a lion, carved out of soft dry wood that looked like spongecake; heraldic, black and, white, with impressionistic detail burnt in. The old man held it up to her still smiling, not from the heart, but at the customer. Between its Vandyke[3] teeth, in the mouth opened in an endless roar too terrible to be heard, it had a black tongue. Look, said the young husband, if you don't mind! And round the neck of the thing, a piece of fur (rat? rabbit? meerkat?); a real mane, majestic, telling you somehow that the artist had delight in the lion.

All up and down the length of the train in the dust the artists sprang, walking bent, like performing animals, the better to exhibit the fantasy held toward the faces on the train. Buck, startled and stiff, staring with round black and white eyes. More lions, standing erect, grappling with strange, thin, elongated warriors who clutched spears and showed no fear in their slits of eyes. How much, they asked from the train, how much?

Give me penny, said the little ones with nothing to sell. The dogs went and sat, quite still, under the dining car, where the train breathed out the smell of meat cooking with onion.

A man passed beneath the arch of reaching arms meeting gray-black and white in the exchange of money for the staring wooden eyes, the stiff wooden legs sticking up in the air; went along under the voices and the bargaining, interrogating the wheels. Past the dogs; glancing up at the dining car where he could stare at the faces, behind glass, drinking beer, two by two, on either side of a uniform railway

---

3. **Vandyke** (van dīk´) *adj.* tapering to a point, like a Vandyke beard.

vase with its pale dead flower. Right to the end, to the guard's van, where the stationmaster's children had just collected their mother's two loaves of bread; to the engine itself, where the stationmaster and the driver stood talking against the steaming complaint of the resting beast.

The man called out to them, something loud and joking. They turned to laugh, in a twirl of steam. The two children careered over the sand, clutching the bread, and burst through the iron gate and up the path through the garden in which nothing grew.

Passengers drew themselves in at the corridor windows and turned into compartments to fetch money, to call someone to look. Those sitting inside looked up: suddenly different, caged faces, boxed in, cut off, after the contact of outside. There was an orange a piccanin would like. . . . What about that chocolate? It wasn't very nice. . . .

A young girl had collected a handful of the hard kind, that no one liked, out of the chocolate box, and was throwing them to the dogs, over at the dining car. But the hens darted in, and swallowed the chocolates, incredibly quick and accurate, before they had even dropped in the dust, and the dogs, a little bewildered, looked up with their brown eyes, not expecting anything.

—No, leave it, said the girl, don't take it. . . .

Too expensive, too much, she shook her head and raised her voice to the old boy, giving up the lion. He held it high where she had handed it to him. No, she said, shaking her head. Three-and-six?[4] insisted her husband, loudly. Yes baas! laughed the old man. Three-and-six? —The young man was incredulous. Oh leave it—she said. The young man stopped. Don't you want it? he said, keeping his face closed to the old man. No, never mind, she said, leave it. The old native kept his head on one side, looking at them sideways, holding the lion. Three-and-six, he murmured, as old people repeat things to themselves.

The young woman drew her head in. She went into the coupé[5] and sat down. Out of the window, on the

---

4. three-and-six three shillings and sixpence.

5. coupé (koo pā′) *n.* half-compartment at the end of a train, with seats on only one side.

TAKE NOTES

other side, there was nothing; sand and bush; a thorn tree. Back through the open doorway, past the figure of her husband in the corridor, there was the station, the voices, wooden animals waving, running feet. Her eye followed the funny little valance of scrolled wood that outlined the chalet roof of the station; she thought of the lion and smiled. That bit of fur round the neck. But the wooden buck, the hippos, the elephants, the baskets that already bulked out of their brown paper under the seat and on the luggage rack! How will they look at home? Where will you put them? What will they mean away from the places you found them? Away from the unreality of the last few weeks? The young man outside. But he is not part of the unreality; he is for good now. Odd . . . somewhere there was an idea that he, that living with him, was part of the holiday, the strange places.

Outside, a bell rang. The stationmaster was leaning against the end of the train, green flag rolled in readiness. A few men who had got down to stretch their legs sprang onto the train, clinging to the observation platforms, or perhaps merely standing on the iron step, holding the rail; but on the train, safe from the one dusty platform, the one tin house, the empty sand.

There was a grunt. The train jerked. Through the glass the beer drinkers looked out, as if they could not see beyond it. Behind the flyscreen, the stationmaster's wife sat facing back at them beneath the darkening hunk of meat.

There was a shout. The flag drooped out. Joints not yet coordinated, the segmented body of the train heaved and bumped back against itself. It began to move; slowly the scrolled chalet moved past it, the yells of the natives, running alongside, jetted up into the air, fell back at different levels. Staring wooden faces waved drunkenly, there, then gone, questioning for the last time at the windows. Here, one-and-six baas!—As one automatically opens a hand to catch a thrown ball, a man fumbled wildly down his pocket, brought up the shilling and sixpence and threw them out; the old native, gasping, his skinny toes splaying the sand, flung the lion.

The piccanins were waving, the dogs stood, tails uncertain, watching the train go: past the mud huts, where a woman turned to look, up from the smoke of the fire, her hand pausing on her hip.

The stationmaster went slowly in under the chalet.

The old native stood, breath blowing out the skin between his ribs, feet tense, balanced in the sand, smiling and shaking his head. In his opened palm, held in the attitude of receiving, was the retrieved shilling and sixpence.

The blind end of the train was being pulled helplessly out of the station.

The young man swung in from the corridor, breathless. He was shaking his head with laughter and triumph. Here! he said. And waggled the lion at her. One-and-six!

What? she said.

He laughed. I was arguing with him for fun, bargaining—when the train had pulled out already, he came tearing after. . . . One-and-six baas! So there's your lion.

She was holding it away from her, the head with the open jaws, the pointed teeth, the black tongue, the wonderful ruff of fur facing her. She was looking at it with an expression of not seeing, of seeing something different. Her face was drawn up, wryly, like the face of a discomforted child. Her mouth lifted nervously at the corner. Very slowly, cautious, she lifted her finger and touched the mane, where it was joined to the wood.

But how could you, she said. He was shocked by the dismay of her face.

Good Lord, he said, what's the matter?

If you wanted the thing, she said, her voice rising and breaking with the shrill impotence of anger, why didn't you buy it in the first place? If you wanted it, why didn't you pay for it?

Why didn't you take it decently, when he offered it? Why did you have to wait for him to run after the train with it, and give him one-and-six? One-and-six!

She was pushing it at him, trying to force him to take it. He stood astonished, his hands hanging at his sides.

But you wanted it! You liked it so much?

—It's a beautiful piece of work, she said fiercely, as if to protect it from him.

TAKE NOTES

You liked it so much! You said yourself it was too expensive—

Oh you—she said, hopeless and furious. You. . . . She threw the lion onto the seat.

He stood looking at her.

She sat down again in the corner and, her face slumped in her hand, stared out of the window. Everything was turning around inside her. One-and-six. One-and-six. One-and-six for the wood and the carving and the sinews of the legs and the switch of the tail. The mouth open like that and the teeth. The black tongue, rolling, like a wave. The mane round the neck. To give one-and-six for that. The heat of shame mounted through her legs and body and sounded in her ears like the sound of sand pouring. Pouring, pouring. She sat there, sick. A weariness, a tastelessness, the discovery of a void made her hands slacken their grip, atrophy emptily, as if the hour was not worth their grasp. She was feeling like this again. She had thought it was something to do with singleness, with being alone and belonging too much to oneself.

She sat there not wanting to move or speak, or to look at anything, even; so that the mood should be associated with nothing, no object, word or sight that might recur and so recall the feeling again. . . . Smuts blew in grittily, settled on her hands. Her back remained at exactly the same angle, turned against the young man sitting with his hands drooping between his sprawled legs, and the lion, fallen on its side in the corner.

The train had cast the station like a skin. It called out to the sky, I'm coming, I'm coming; and again, there was no answer.

A Devoted Son

by Anita Desai

BACKGROUND *Since India won its independence from Britain in 1947, modernization has resulted in dramatic contrasts between old and new. In this story, Anita Desai dramatizes the conflict between the traditional respect shown parents, symbolized in the custom of touching one's father's feet, and the modern education that parents strive for their children to acquire.*

When the results appeared in the morning papers, Rakesh scanned them barefoot and in his pajamas, at the garden gate, then went up the steps to the verandah[1] where his father sat sipping his morning tea and bowed down to touch his feet.

"A first division, son?" his father asked, beaming, reaching for the papers.

"At the top of the list, papa," Rakesh murmured, as if awed. "First in the country."

Bedlam broke loose then. The family whooped and danced. The whole day long visitors streamed into the small yellow house at the end of the road to congratulate the parents of this *Wunderkind*,[2] to slap Rakesh on the back and fill the house and garden with the sounds and colors of a festival. There were garlands and halwa,[3] party clothes and gifts (enough fountain pens to last years, even a watch or two), nerves and temper and joy, all in a multicolored whirl of pride and great shining vistas newly opened: Rakesh was the first son in the family to receive an education, so much had been sacrificed in order to send him to school and then medical college, and at

---

1. **verandah** (və ran´də) *n.* partly enclosed porch or balcony along the outside of a building; also spelled veranda.
2. ***Wunderkind*** (voon´dər kint´) *n.* person who achieves remarkable success at an early age.
3. **halwa** (häl vä´) *n.* Middle Eastern sweet made from sesame flour and honey; also spelled halvah or halva.

TAKE NOTES

last the fruits of their sacrifice had arrived, golden and glorious.

To everyone who came to him to say "*Mubarak*,[4] Varmaji, your son has brought you glory," the father said, "Yes, and do you know what is the first thing he did when he saw the results this morning? He came and touched my feet. He bowed down and touched my feet." This moved many of the women in the crowd so much that they were seen to raise the ends of their saris[5] and dab at their tears while the men reached out for the betel-leaves[6] and sweetmeats that were offered around on trays and shook their heads in wonder and approval of such exemplary filial behavior. "One does not often see such behavior in sons any more," they all agreed, a little enviously perhaps. Leaving the house, some of the women said, sniffing, "At least on such an occasion they might have served pure *ghee*[7] sweets," and some of the men said, "Don't you think old Varma was giving himself airs? He needn't think we don't remember that he comes from the vegetable market himself, his father used to sell vegetables, and he has never seen the inside of a school." But there was more envy than rancor in their voices and it was, of course, inevitable—not every son in that shabby little colony at the edge of the city was destined to shine as Rakesh shone, and who knew that better than the parents themselves?

And that was only the beginning, the first step in a great, sweeping ascent to the radiant heights of fame and fortune. The thesis he wrote for his M.D. brought Rakesh still greater glory, if only in select medical circles. He won a scholarship. He went to the USA (that was what his father learnt to call it and taught the whole family to say—not America, which was what the ignorant neighbors called it, but, with a grand familiarity, "the USA") where he pursued his career in the most prestigious of all hospitals and won encomiums from his American colleagues which

---

4. **Mubarak** (mu bär´ək) greeting meaning "blessed one." The word, originally from Arabic, has become part of some languages spoken in India.
5. **saris** (sä´rēz) *n.* traditional garments worn by Indian women, consisting of lengths of cotton, silk, or other cloth wrapped around the waist and draped over one shoulder.
6. **betel-leaves** (bēt´l) *n.* leaves from an evergreen shrub, usually wrapped around seeds from that shrub and commonly chewed in Asia.
7. **ghee** (gē) *n.* clarified butter, often used in Indian cooking.

were relayed to his admiring and glowing family. What was more, he came *back*, he actually returned to that small yellow house in the once-new but increasingly shabby colony, right at the end of the road where the rubbish vans[8] tipped out their stinking contents for pigs to nose in and rag-pickers to build their shacks on, all steaming and smoking just outside the neat wire fences and welltended gardens. To this Rakesh returned and the first thing he did on entering the house was to slip out of the embraces of his sisters and brothers and bow down and touch his father's feet.

As for his mother, she gloated chiefly over the strange fact that he had not married in America, had not brought home a foreign wife as all her neighbors had warned her he would, for wasn't that what all Indian boys went abroad for? Instead he agreed, almost without argument, to marry a girl she had picked out for him in her own village, the daughter of a childhood friend, a plump and uneducated girl, it was true, but so old-fashioned, so placid, so complaisant that she slipped into the household and settled in like a charm, seemingly too lazy and too good-natured to even try and make Rakesh leave home and set up independently, as any other girl might have done. What was more, she was pretty—really pretty, in a plump, pudding way that only gave way to fat—soft, spreading fat, like warm wax—after the birth of their first baby, a son, and then what did it matter?

For some years Rakesh worked in the city hospital, quickly rising to the top of the administrative organization, and was made a director before he left to set up his own clinic. He took his parents in his car—a new, sky-blue Ambassador[9] with a rear window full of stickers and charms revolving on strings—to see the clinic when it was built, and the large sign-board over the door on which his name was printed in letters of red, with a row of degrees and qualifications to follow it like so many little black slaves of the regent.[10] Thereafter his fame seemed to grow just a little dimmer—or maybe it was only that everyone in town had grown accustomed to it at last—but it was

---

   8. rubbish vans garbage trucks.
   9. Ambassador popular model of car manufactured by Hindustan Motors of India.
   10. regent (rē′jənt) *n.* ruler; governor.

TAKE NOTES

also the beginning of his fortune for he now became known not only as the best but also the richest doctor in town.

However, all this was not accomplished in the wink of an eye. Naturally not. It was the achievement of a lifetime and it took up Rakesh's whole life. At the time he set up his clinic his father had grown into an old man and retired from his post at the kerosene dealer's depot at which he had worked for forty years, and his mother died soon after, giving up the ghost with a sigh that sounded positively happy, for it was her own son who ministered to her in her last illness and who sat pressing her feet at the last moment—such a son as few women had borne.

For it had to be admitted—and the most unsuccessful and most rancorous of neighbors eventually did so—that Rakesh was not only a devoted son and a miraculously good-natured man who contrived somehow to obey his parents and humor his wife and show concern equally for his children and his patients, but there was actually a brain inside this beautifully polished and formed body of good manners and kind nature and, in between ministering to his family and playing host to many friends and coaxing them all into feeling happy and grateful and content, he had actually trained his hands as well and emerged an excellent doctor, a really fine surgeon. How one man—and a man born to illiterate parents, his father having worked for a kerosene dealer and his mother having spent her life in a kitchen—had achieved, combined and conducted such a medley of virtues, no one could fathom, but all acknowledged his talent and skill.

It was a strange fact, however, that talent and skill, if displayed for too long, cease to dazzle. It came to pass that the most admiring of all eyes eventually faded and no longer blinked at his glory. Having retired from work and having lost his wife, the old father very quickly went to pieces, as they say. He developed so many complaints and fell ill so frequently and with such mysterious diseases that even his son could no longer make out when it was something of significance and when it was merely a peevish whim. He sat huddled on his string bed most of the day

and developed an exasperating habit of stretching
out suddenly and lying absolutely still, allowing the
whole family to fly around him in a flap, wailing and
weeping, and then suddenly sitting up, stiff and
gaunt, and spitting out a big gob of betel-juice as if to
mock their behavior.

He did this once too often: there had been a big
party in the house, a birthday party for the youngest
son, and the celebrations had to be suddenly hushed,
covered up and hustled out of the way when the
daughter-in-law discovered, or thought she discovered,
that the old man, stretched out from end to end of his
string bed, had lost his pulse; the party broke up,
dissolved, even turned into a band of mourners, when
the old man sat up and the distraught daughter-in-
law received a gob of red spittle right on the hem of her
organza[11] sari. After that no one much cared if he sat
up crosslegged on his bed, hawking and spitting, or
lay down flat and turned gray as a corpse. Except, of
course, for that pearl amongst pearls, his son Rakesh.

It was Rakesh who brought him his morning tea,
not in one of the china cups from which the rest of
the family drank, but in the old man's favorite brass
tumbler, and sat at the edge of his bed, comfortable
and relaxed with the string of his pajamas dangling
out from under his fine lawn night-shirt, and
discussed or, rather, read out the morning news to
his father. It made no difference to him that his father
made no response apart from spitting. It was Rakesh,
too, who, on returning from the clinic in the evening,
persuaded the old man to come out of his room, as
bare and desolate as a cell, and take the evening air
out in the garden, beautifully arranging the pillows
and bolsters on the divan[12] in the corner of the open
verandah. On summer nights he saw to it that the
servants carried out the old man's bed onto the lawn
and himself helped his father down the steps and onto
the bed, soothing him and settling him down for a night
under the stars.

All this was very gratifying for the old man. What

---

11. **organza** (ôr gan´ze) *n.* stiff sheer fabric.
12. **divan** (de´van´ or di van´) *n.* long backless sofa on which pillows or bolsters are
usually arranged to support the back.

TAKE NOTES

TAKE NOTES

was not so gratifying was that he even undertook to supervise his father's diet. One day when the father was really sick, having ordered his daughter-in-law to make him a dish of *soojie*[13] *halwa* and eaten it with a saucerful of cream, Rakesh marched into the room, not with his usual respectful step but with the confident and rather contemptuous stride of the famous doctor, and declared, "No more *halwa* for you, papa. We must be sensible, at your age. If you must have something sweet, Veena will cook you a little *kheer*,[14] that's light, just a little rice and milk. But nothing fried, nothing rich. We can't have this happening again."

The old man who had been lying stretched out on his bed, weak and feeble after a day's illness, gave a start at the very sound, the tone of these words. He opened his eyes—rather, they fell open with shock—and he stared at his son with disbelief that darkened quickly to reproach. A son who actually refused his father the food he craved? No, it was unheard of, it was incredible. But Rakesh had turned his back to him and was cleaning up the litter of bottles and packets on the medicine shelf and did not notice while Veena slipped silently out of the room with a little smirk that only the old man saw, and hated.

Halwa was only the first item to be crossed off the old man's diet. One delicacy after the other went—everything fried to begin with, then everything sweet, and eventually everything, everything that the old man enjoyed.

The meals that arrived for him on the shining stainless steel tray twice a day were frugal to say the least—dry bread, boiled lentils, boiled vegetables and, if there were a bit of chicken or fish, that was boiled too. If he called for another helping—in a cracked voice that quavered theatrically—Rakesh himself would come to the door, gaze at him sadly and shake his head, saying, "Now, papa, we must be careful, we can't risk another illness, you know," and although the daughter-in-law kept tactfully out of the way, the old man could just see her smirk sliding merrily

---

13. **soojie** *n.* Indian term for semolina, a coarse grain usually made from wheat; often spelled sooji or suji.

14. **kheer** (kir) *n.* rice pudding traditionally served as a dessert in southern India.

through the air. He tried to bribe his grandchildren into buying him sweets (and how he missed his wife now, that generous, indulgent and illiterate cook), whispering, "Here's fifty paise,"[15] as he stuffed the coins into a tight, hot fist. "Run down to the shop at the crossroads and buy me thirty paise worth of *jalebis*,[16] and you can spend the remaining twenty paise on yourself. Eh? Understand? Will you do that?" He got away with it once or twice but then was found out, the conspirator was scolded by his father and smacked by his mother and Rakesh came storming into the room, almost tearing his hair as he shouted through compressed lips, "Now papa, are you trying to turn my little son into a liar? Quite apart from spoiling your own stomach, you are spoiling him as well—you are encouraging him to lie to his own parents. You should have heard the lies he told his mother when she saw him bringing back those *jalebis* wrapped up in filthy newspaper. I don't allow anyone in my house to buy sweets in the bazaar,[17] papa, surely you know that. There's cholera[18] in the city, typhoid, gastroenteritis—I see these cases daily in the hospital, how can I allow my own family to run such risks?" The old man sighed and lay down in the corpse position. But that worried no one any longer.

There was only one pleasure left in the old man now (his son's early morning visits and readings from the newspaper could no longer be called that) and those were visits from elderly neighbors. These were not frequent as his contemporaries were mostly as decrepit and helpless as he and few could walk the length of the road to visit him any more. Old Bhatia, next door, however, who was still spry enough to refuse, adamantly, to bathe in the tiled bathroom indoors and to insist on carrying out his brass mug and towel, in all seasons and usually at impossible hours, into the yard and bathe noisily under the garden tap, would look over the hedge to see if Varma were out on his verandah and would call to him and

---

15. **paise** (pī̆ se) *n.* plural of paisa, Indian money equal to 1/100 of a rupee.
16. *jalebis* (jä leb'ēz) *n.* Indian sweets made by frying a coil of batter and then soaking it in syrup.
17. **bazaar** (bə zär') *n.* open-air market.
18. **cholera** (käl'ər ə) . . . **typhoid** (tī'foid), **gastroenteritis** dangerous infectious diseases causing fever or intestinal problems.

TAKE NOTES

talk while he wrapped his *dhoti*[19] about him and dried the sparse hair on his head, shivering with enjoyable exaggeration. Of course these conversations, bawled across the hedge by two rather deaf old men conscious of having their entire households overhearing them, were not very satisfactory but Bhatia occasionally came out of his yard, walked down the bit of road and came in at Varma's gate to collapse onto the stone plinth built under the temple tree.[20] If Rakesh was at home he would help his father down the steps into the garden and arrange him on his night bed under the tree and leave the two old men to chew betel-leaves and discuss the ills of their individual bodies with combined passion.

"At least you have a doctor in the house to look after you," sighed Bhatia, having vividly described his martyrdom to piles.[21]

"Look after me?" cried Varma, his voice cracking like an ancient clay jar. "He—he does not even give me enough to eat."

"What?" said Bhatia, the white hairs in his ears twitching. "Doesn't give you enough to eat? Your own son?"

"My own son. If I ask him for one more piece of bread, he says no, papa, I weighed out the *ata*[22] myself and I can't allow you to have more than two hundred grams of cereal a day. He *weighs* the food he gives me, Bhatia—he has scales to weigh it on. That is what it has come to."

"Never," murmured Bhatia in disbelief. "Is it possible, even in this evil age, for a son to refuse his father food?"

"Let me tell you," Varma whispered eagerly. "Today the family was having fried fish—I could smell it. I called to my daughter-in-law to bring me a piece. She came to the door and said no. . . ."

"Said no?" It was Bhatia's voice that cracked. A *drongo*[23] shot out of the tree and sped away. *"No?"*

---

19. *dhoti* (dō′tē) *n.* cloth worn by Hindu men in India, with the ends passing through the legs and tucked in at the waist.
20. **stone . . . tree** stone slab beneath the frangipani, an erect tree often grown in temple gardens in India.
21. **piles** *n.* hemorrhoids.
22. **ata** (ä′tə) *n.* type of flour used in India.
23. **drongo** *n.* black bird with a long forked tail.

"No, she said no, Rakesh has ordered her to give me nothing fried. No butter, he says, no oil. . . ."

"No butter? No oil? How does he expect his father to live?"

Old Varma nodded with melancholy triumph. "That is how he treats me—after I have brought him up, given him an education, made him a great doctor. Great doctor! This is the way great doctors treat their fathers, Bhatia," for the son's sterling personality and character now underwent a curious sea change. Outwardly all might be the same but the interpretation had altered: his masterly efficiency was nothing but cold heartlessness, his authority was only tyranny in disguise.

There was cold comfort in complaining to neighbors and, on such a miserable diet, Varma found himself slipping, weakening and soon becoming a genuinely sick man. Powders and pills and mixtures were not only brought in when dealing with a crisis like an upset stomach but became a regular part of his diet— became his diet, complained Varma, supplanting the natural foods he craved. There were pills to regulate his bowel movements, pills to bring down his blood pressure, pills to deal with his arthritis and, eventually, pills to keep his heart beating. In between there were panicky rushes to the hospital, some humiliating experience with the stomach pump and enema, which left him frightened and helpless. He cried easily, shriveling up on his bed, but if he complained of a pain or even a vague, gray fear in the night, Rakesh would simply open another bottle of pills and force him to take one. "I have my duty to you papa," he said when his father begged to be let off.

"Let me be," Varma begged, turning his face away from the pills on the outstretched hand. "Let me die. It would be better. I do not want to live only to eat your medicines."

"Papa, be reasonable."

"I leave that to you," the father cried with sudden spirit. "Leave me alone, let me die now, I cannot live like this."

"Lying all day on his pillows, fed every few hours by his daughter-in-law's own hand, visited by every

TAKE NOTES

member of his family daily—and then he says he does not want to live 'like this,'" Rakesh was heard to say, laughing, to someone outside the door.

"Deprived of food," screamed the old man on the bed, "his wishes ignored, taunted by his daughter-in-law, laughed at by his grandchildren—*that* is how I live." But he was very old and weak and all anyone heard was an incoherent croak, some expressive grunts and cries of genuine pain. Only once, when old Bhatia had come to see him and they sat together under the temple tree, they heard him cry, "God is calling me—and they won't let me go."

The quantities of vitamins and tonics he was made to take were not altogether useless. They kept him alive and even gave him a kind of strength that made him hang on long after he ceased to wish to hang on. It was as though he were straining at a rope, trying to break it, and it would not break, it was still strong. He only hurt himself, trying.

In the evening, that summer, the servants would come into his cell, grip his bed, one at each end, and carry it out to the verandah, there sitting it down with a thump that jarred every tooth in his head. In answer to his agonized complaints they said the doctor sahib[24] had told them he must take the evening air and the evening air they would make him take—thump. Then Veena, that smiling, hypocritical pudding in a rustling sari, would appear and pile up the pillows under his head till he was propped up stiffly into a sitting position that made his head swim and his back ache.

"Let me lie down," he begged. "I can't sit up any more."

"Try, papa, Rakesh said you can if you try," she said, and drifted away to the other end of the verandah where her transistor radio vibrated to the lovesick tunes from the cinema[25] that she listened to all day.

So there he sat, like some stiff corpse, terrified, gazing out on the lawn where his grandsons played cricket,[26] in danger of getting one of their hard-spun balls in his eye, and at the gate that opened onto the dusty and rubbish-heaped lane but still bore,

---

24. **sahib** (sä´ib´, hib´, ēb´, or hĭ´b´) Indian term of respect.
25. **cinema** (sin´ə mə) *n.* movies.
26. **cricket** *n.* open-air game played between two teams using balls and bats.

proudly, a newly touched-up signboard that bore his son's name and qualifications, his own name having vanished from the gate long ago.

At last the sky-blue Ambassador arrived, the cricket game broke up in haste, the car drove in smartly and the doctor, the great doctor, all in white, stepped out. Someone ran up to take his bag from him, others to escort him up the steps. "Will you have tea?" his wife called, turning down the transistor set. "Or a Coca-Cola? Shall I fry you some *samosas*?"[27] But he did not reply or even glance in her direction. Ever a devoted son, he went first to the corner where his father sat gazing, stricken, at some undefined spot in the dusty yellow air that swam before him. He did not turn his head to look at his son. But he stopped gobbling air with his uncontrolled lips and set his jaw as hard as a sick and very old man could set it.

"Papa," his son said, tenderly, sitting down on the edge of the bed and reaching out to press his feet.

Old Varma tucked his feet under him, out of the way, and continued to gaze stubbornly into the yellow air of the summer evening.

"Papa, I'm home."

Varma's hand jerked suddenly, in a sharp, derisive movement, but he did not speak.

"How are you feeling, papa?"

Then Varma turned and looked at his son. His face was so out of control and all in pieces, that the multitude of expressions that crossed it could not make up a whole and convey to the famous man exactly what his father thought of him, his skill, his art.

"I'm dying," he croaked. "Let me die, I tell you."

"Papa, you're joking," his son smiled at him, lovingly. "I've brought you a new tonic to make you feel better. You must take it, it will make you feel stronger again. Here it is. Promise me you will take it regularly, papa."

Varma's mouth worked as hard as though he still had a gob of betel in it (his supply of betel had been cut off years ago). Then he spat out some words, as sharp and bitter as poison, into his son's face. "Keep

---

27. samosas (sə mō´səz) *n.* fried triangular Indian pastries containing vegetables or meat.

TAKE NOTES

your tonic—I want none—I want none—I won't take any more of—of your medicines. None. Never," and he swept the bottle out of his son's hand with a wave of his own, suddenly grand, suddenly effective.

His son jumped, for the bottle was smashed and thick brown syrup had splashed up, staining his white trousers. His wife let out a cry and came running. All around the old man was hubbub once again, noise, attention.

He gave one push to the pillows at his back and dislodged them so he could sink down on his back, quite flat again. He closed his eyes and pointed his chin at the ceiling, like some dire prophet, groaning, "God is calling me—now let me go."

Grateful acknowledgment is made to the following for copyrighted material:

Dutton Signet From *Beowulf* by Burton Raffel, translator. Translation copyright © 1963, renewed © 1991 by Burton Raffel. Used by permission of Dutton Signet, a division of Penguin Group (USA) Inc.

W. W. Norton & Company, Inc. "The Inferno: Canto XXXIV", from *The Divine Comedy* by Dante Alighieri, translated by John Ciardi. Copyright 1954, 1957, 1959, 1960, 1961, 1965, 1967, 1970 by the Ciardi Family Publishing Trust.

Penguin Books Ltd., London "The Wife of Bath's Tale" from *The Canterbury Tales* by Geoffrey Chaucer, translated by Nevill Coghill (Penguin Classics 1951, Fourth revised edition 1977). Copyright 1951 by Nevill Coghill. Copyright © the Estate of Nevill Coghill, 1958, 1960, 1975, 1977.

Rogers, Coleridge & White Ltd. "A Devoted Son" from *Games at Twilight and Other Stories* by Anita Desai. Copyright © 1978 Anita Desai. Reproduced by permission of the author c/o Rogers, Coleridge & White Ltd., 20 Powis Mews, London W11 1JN.

Russell & Volkening, Inc. "The Train from Rhodesia" from *Selected Stories* by Nadine Gordimer. Copyright © 1950 by Nadine Gordimer, renewed in 1978 by Nadine Gordimer. Used by the permission of Russell & Volkening as agents for the author.

Yale University Press "The Seafarer" from *Poems from the Old English*, translated by Burton Raffel. Copyright © 1960, 1964; renewed 1988, 1922 by The University of Nebraska Press. Copyright © 1994 by Burton Raffel. Used by permission of Yale University Press.

Note: Every effort has been made to locate the copyright owner of material reproduced on this component. Omissions brought to our attention will be corrected in subsequent editions.